JESUS IS THE TITHE

The Message of God

Bertie Brits

Table of Contents

Acknowledgment

It is not easy to preach a message that is not widely accepted in the church while what you preach seems not to work in the eyes of those that don't agree with you. My wife, Helena, and our three sons stood with me and gave their full support to me in these times, which I am grateful for.

The Father Son and Holy Spirit for revealing the truths, contained in this book, to me.

About the Author

Bertie and Helena Brits are the founders of Dynamic Love Ministries. They are based in South Africa from where they reach out to the rest of the world. Bertie has been preaching the Gospel of Jesus since 1992, having his focus and passion towards the message of Grace, since it is the only way unto the victory that God has planned for man. In his early years he planted churches in Southern Africa and conducted hundreds of open-air Gospel outreaches in which thousands of people came to know the message of God's love for them.

In the Brits' internet-based Dynamic Love Web Church, many people are reached all over the world by weekly messages and grace-based fellowship via the web. Since 2007, Bertie has had a weekly program on television where he has had a major impact on many people. He also pastors two local churches in his area.

The major focus of Bertie's ministry is the Trinity, from where he has a family-based approach to the Gospel, which you will encounter in a powerful way in this book.

Foreword

The Mind blowing Gospel of Jesus Christ

There is unending good news in what God accomplished in Jesus. Jesus did a work so grand that the human mind needs assistance from God Himself to comprehend it. What God accomplished in Jesus blows what Satan did in Adam completely out of the water!

God's original plan with man was to have a friend with whom He could share His life. When He made man, He wasn't driven by a business decision to hire a gardener for the Garden of Eden. The creation of man is based on the same passions, thoughts and qualities displayed in the life of a loving married couple who want children with whom they could share all they have.

What drives the Trinity is their passion for serving a person with life, and to see their image and likeness inside someone who is born from their union. The passion God has for us can be likened to loving, caring parents that are driven to make sandwiches for their children's school day, and to provide for them however they can. Just as parents are driven by a passion to share their life with their children, this is the beautiful reason why God had us. I can imagine God walking in the Garden of Eden, in the cool of the day, laughing, talking and joking within the Trinity. You could hear them a mile away, as they lovingly shared their lives in perfect union with each other, a union in which they also included Adam and Eve. I think God is talkative; He is fun to be around and loves life. I think He is so talkative that we can call Him "the Word," without offending Him.

When God made Adam from the dust of the Earth, He gave him the ability to be alive and to have a living relationship with Him. All life would flow from this relationship. Adam became the very place where God displayed all His goodness. Adam and Eve were the objects of God's love, which was their very source of life. As Adam believed in God, his heart was opened to all the life of God for him. He did not have to produce life; life was a gift. When we read the Genesis account of God's relationship with Adam, we can see what I'm talking about—but then something happened:

8 *And they heard the voice of the LORD God walking in the garden in the cool of the day: and Adam and his wife hid themselves from the presence of the LORD God amongst the trees of the garden.*
9 *And the LORD God called unto Adam, and said unto him, Where art thou?* (*KJV*, Gen. 3:8, 9).

When Adam and Eve heard God talking and laughing from afar, they hid themselves, and it was then that God called for them. God's call to Adam must've sounded like any father's cry for a son who's gone missing, full of care and concern—not anger or wrath. Yet, many of us picture the fall of mankind as if God came to 'pay Adam a visit'—so to speak—as soon as He found out about his mistake. I don't believe that is what happened.

The Bible documents God's visit with Adam and Eve as just an ordinary day in paradise, not God hunting them down to confront and punish them! We can only imagine the wonderful, fearless fellowship there must've been in the garden between Father, Son, Holy Spirit, Adam and Eve, prior to the fall. When God visited Adam and Eve, He did not come to take an inventory of the work they had accomplished each day. It was not about "Boss God" coming to see if His garden was okay; He came simply longing to see if His friends were okay.

We should never think of God as anything other than love and family. God is a family, and we are invited to pull up a chair and sit with Him at His table of love and fellowship, within the Trinity. As we dwell in the presence of such a good God, beholding the love in the Trinity, we can't help but to be influenced by it. God's desire has always been to bear His fruit in us, thus sharing His quality of life with us as a free gift. He longs to give you all that He has, and for you to share in feeling the birth of generosity in your own heart. His care *for* you will be the birth *in* you of one who cares effortlessly for others. He will love you into being a lover. This is how He planned to live in you. By Him doing this, we experience His wonderful life, the life from where all good things come forth. As the Father is one with His Son, He is also one with us. We will forever be His kind, and that He will never forget.

When Adam fell, he never lost his value nor his beauty.

Something very deadly and cruel grabbed ahold of Adam. I can see the concern in the heart of Father, Son, and Holy Spirit at that moment. When death grabbed ahold of Adam, it wasn't God thinking of ways to kill him. Adam placed himself in death's grip when he chose to go his own way. There was no reason for God to kill a man who was already being killed by the deadly Tree of the Knowledge of Good and Evil. When God warned Adam not to eat of the tree, He warned him that the fruit of the tree would kill him, not that God would kill him out of anger for not being obedient.

God could only think of ways to redeem Adam, even if it meant dying in his place. When a child disobeys, the father of the child is still his father. When something valuable is stolen, its owner still owns it and its value has not changed!

Just as the prodigal son was a lost son, yet still very much his father's son, all people—while lost into what is killing them—are still very much God's people. The channel by which this death found its way into the life of Adam, Eve, and all of humanity, was the abandonment of trust in God for trust in the Tree of the Knowledge of Good and Evil. The valuable, beautiful man and woman, who were the Godkind, became slaves of sin and death. Through Adam's fatal choice, mankind was bound to the Tree of Death. From that moment on, our loving Father has demonstrated His love and His very being, in all shapes and forms, to get man back to a place of life and peace that could last forever, ultimately accomplished in the death and resurrection of Jesus.

Wouldn't any loving father want to save his son from

death? God has never been self-seeking, unloving, unfriendly, resentful, or keeping score of sin. The self-giving, generous, loving and caring God (Father, Son and Holy Spirit) has never changed and will never change. The power of our Salvation is born from the love there is in the Trinity.

What could be so deadly about the Tree of the Knowledge of Good and Evil that it could destroy man? Let's have a deeper look at that tree. The Septuagint is the Greek Old Testament, read by Paul and others who lived in the days of Jesus. The following definitions for the words *good* and *evil* are taken from the Greek Septuagint:

Good and Evil
Good
Kalos
Thayer Definition:

1) **beautiful**, handsome, **excellent**, eminent, choice, surpassing, **precious**, useful, suitable, **commendable, admirable**

Evil

ponēros

Thayer Definition:

1) **full of labours**, annoyances, hardships
1a) **pressed and harassed by labors; from the root word - strong desire**

I am going to keep it simple: eating from the Tree of the Knowledge of Good and Evil is believing a good life is obtained by **trying to work the good we see in God**. From this **works principle** we can even write a list of laws on how to have life. All you need to do is look at God and how good He is, start trying to do all the good things you see in God, and have life by working the good. Here is an example of such a list of laws:

- Love all people
- Love God with all your heart
- Be a giver
- Be friendly
- Sacrifice yourself
- Be willing to be the least
- Don't steal
- Be kind
- The list goes on and on …

By looking at this list we can all see the focus will be on **us** to produce good works. There is nothing wrong with the list, yet it will be completely ineffective in bringing forth life in us! Even if we take all the holiness of God and put it in writing, a list of perfect rules from beholding God's quality of life will be powerless. Why is this? This is because **life is not found in good works, but good works come from the life**. In other words, if you have God's life, then good works will manifest. But, life cannot be created by good works.

The more you try to find life by obedience to rules, the less you will find it. You will experience death. When we eat of the Tree of Knowledge of Good and Evil, death knocks at the door. Who would ever think that a tree flourishing in the beauty of God could be the root of all death! While it was beautiful because of God's supply, mixing in the belief that one must work all those good things in order to have life meant death for all who partook of it.

Adam ate of this tree and entered death, leading to the complete destruction of all human beings. The beautiful, lovely people of God would all die now, because of that tree. The poison of *life by works* was killing man, so that life could not be called *life* anymore; it is now called, "death unto death" (See 2 Cor. 2:16). All will die and no one will be left alive. In the heart of the powerful God-family (Father, Son and Holy Spirit), was the loving answer to mankind's problem. They had to bring about the death of all people, so we could all have the opportunity to live. Is this even possible? Can there really be such a plan? Yes, and a million times yes!

What God prepared for us in Jesus is more than we can ever ask, think or even imagine! The all-loving God of the universe had the solution inside Himself: He would bring redemption to all people, so that everyone who **believed** could be saved. What would this plan be? How would it look? How would He bring forth the death of all, yet have them live? Very few people know it, but Adam was the son of God. Here is the Scripture that proves it:

"*Which was the son of Enos, which was the son of Seth, which was the son of* ***Adam****, which was* ***the son of God***" (*KJV*, Luke 3:38).

All sin and death came into the world on account of one man, Adam. Adam was acting on behalf of all people. Adam was not Jesus but still a son of God. He was a human being born directly from God. Anyone whose only father is God, has the power of an Adam and is the representative of all people. There have only been two people like that, Adam and Jesus. Jesus was called the *last Adam*:

"And so it is written, The first man Adam was made a living soul; the ***last Adam*** *was made a quickening spirit" (KJV, 1 Cor. 15:45).*

When God looked at all of us, He loved what He saw and could not see His lovely people die. He saw the death from the tree manifesting in us, bringing forth all kinds of fruit of the flesh. Sin spread like a cancer, killing the people God loves. God never confused us with what was happening to us; He loved mankind through it all. He wanted to set us free from the ministration of death (See 2 Cor. 3:6). Then, God's love plan manifested and Jesus was incarnated into human flesh, having God as His Father and being the representative of all people, just like the first Adam.

In bringing forth a last Adam in Jesus, God prepared a body that could die the death of all people. This was possible since Jesus would be in the power of an Adam. If this last Adam could become sin, and sin have its perfect work in His body, all people would die in Him. When the last Adam died and was then raised in human flesh, all people have the hope of life again, as a free gift.

Jesus Christ has redeemed us from what was killing us! The handwriting of laws that was against us was nailed to the cross. The ministration of death, written on stones, was taken out of the way (See 2 Cor. 3:7). God made His life accessible, as a free gift, inside the last Adam, Jesus Christ. All of a sudden, resurrection life, with the Trinity as the foundation of it all, entered the human being who stood in the power of representation for all people. As a human being, He was raised from the dead into eternal life by the Holy Spirit. When Stephen was being stoned to death for preaching the Gospel, he saw that human being raised up to the Father:

"And he said, 'Behold, I see the heavens opened, and the ***Son of Man*** *standing at the right hand of God'" (NKJV, Acts 7:56).*

Whoever receives the Spirit who raised Jesus from the dead, has the promise that the same Spirit will raise them into everlasting life. By not eating of the Tree of the Knowledge of Good and Evil, but instead trusting in Jesus as your life, you will be raised into immortality. This is the GOOD NEWS! Your death has died in Christ and your resurrection is inside Him—not in your performance. **Can you believe it?**

You don't have access to life by eating of the tree that tells you to look at the right thing to do and do it. With this out of the way, all forms of works have been removed and you can now receive His love manifested unto true life. You have the promise of immortality by receiving the Spirit that raised Jesus from the dead. When you believe this truth the Spirit of this truth enters your heart and you are eternally sealed for salvation from death. Even if you die in this world, you will be raised from the dead. As we walk by the Spirit and not by our works, trusting Him for life, we find Salvation manifesting in all forms of the fruit of the Spirit, and in the end, immortality.

In conclusion to this introductory chapter, I would like to

connect this truth to money. Imagine you consider all the good in God. You see His generosity in people's lives; you see that He is always content, never worried, and His great faith and love is expressed in sharing His life with others. As you see this, you notice how people love God back and bless Him in song and giving their lives to Him. A recipe for death would be if you were to analyse the good God has done, then conclude that you will have all that good **by trying to be as good as God and doing what He does**. We don't have life by doing all the good God does! We have life because of what God lovingly accomplishes in us!

If you think copying the good that God does is the key to prosperity and financial blessings, you are in trouble. When you make a list of all the good God has done and see copying Him as the principle by which you will find your breakthrough, you will suffer:

"If I give, live in great faith that all my needs are met, speak positive words, try to stay content, and love people by sowing into their lives and meeting their needs, I will REAP THE GOOD LIFE GOD HAS!!"

This is what I call the ***revelation of death.*** It will destroy your life!

"There is a way that seems right to a man, but its end is the way of death" (NKJV, Prov. 16:25)

A stable future is not found in giving. Contentment, fearless faith, a stable future, and love for others are only found in the life into which God raised Jesus. Only when we believe that His life is our life will we enter eternal life, where we will effortlessly enjoy contentment, peace, stability and love for others. Only then can God bear His fruit in us.

In this book I share my journey out of the misery that lies, dressed in the name of *having life by doing good*, caused in my life. I never thought the way that seemed unto life would destroy me. I will also explain many Bible verses about finances from a grace perspective. Let me share my journey with you.

PART 1

A Relationship-Based Approach to Money in the Kingdom of God

CHAPTER 1

The ABBA in Humanity

(In this chapter I would like to explain that we are the God kind. I will also show you that God has never been alone and has always been a family and that He only operates inside the parameters of family logic.)

- *How can man relate to God?*
- *Is it even possible to have a real relationship with God? What does a meaningful relationship with God call for?*
- *What is the foundation for a relationship between God and man?*
- *Can God fit into our parameters of relating?*
- *Why does man even think he can have a relationship with God?*

I remember a conversation I had with a man sitting next to me on a plane en route to the United States, which was a connecting flight via Dubai. From Cape Town to Dubai, I was fortunate to have an open seat next to me, so I could stretch my legs on the 9-hour flight, and I hoped for the same on the 14-hour flight to New York. As I searched for my seat on the plane in Dubai, I saw there was already someone sitting in the seat next to mine. My first thought was that I would have the opportunity to witness to him on the way, so I introduced myself to the young man, John, and took my seat.

When we reached 10,000 feet and the seat belt sign went off, John started playing games on his cell phone. Five hours later the battery died. Frustrated, John put his phone away and grumbled, "These batteries are terrible. Why can't they make them like they used to, when a Nokia phone could go a week on a single charge!" Then he asked what I do for a living. I have come to realize the worst thing I could ever do, at this point, is to tell the person I'm a pastor. Either it will be the end of all conversation or I will have to deal with an actor for the rest of the flight.

I remember a flight when the person next to me did not ask me once about my occupation, during our seven-hour flight. Then, just before we landed, he asked me. When I answered that I was a pastor, this is what he said, "Why have you not (profanity) warned me!" Obviously, this was a reaction coming directly from the subconscious, not from his cognitive mind. I could clearly see that he connected pastors not only to God, but also to guilt and pain.

I did not want that to happen this time in my conversation with John. So, after he asked me, I told him that I declare the innocence of human beings. When He asked me what I meant, I told him how Adam represented all humanity in sin and Jesus Christ represents all humanity in innocence. He smiled a bit uncomfortably but said that it sounded awesome. There seemed to be a part of him that wanted to hear more, but another part that was afraid and on guard. After I witnessed to him for about 30 minutes, I could clearly see that the message of grace really blessed him.

Then, as we came in for our landing in New York and they told us to switch off our phones, place our seats in the upright position and tighten our safety belts, a phone rang. When I realized it was John's phone and told him so, he looked stressed and said that it couldn't be his, since his phone's battery was completely flat. He also said that it was his first visit to the United States and he had not registered on a U.S. cell phone network.

I suggested, "Then it must be God who wants to speak to you."

John replied, "Then I will never pick up the phone."

When I asked him why, he told me that God would only rebuke him for his bad lifestyle and that he was not ready for that kind of conversation.

John was living in fear towards God. The fear in his heart is a manifestation of a wrong belief about who God really is. Believing God is a sin-conscious God will put you in a place where you want more distance between you and Him. No person has been made to function under scrutiny, rebuke and the fear of punishment. Should a negative picture of God be in your mind when you think of God, it would be very difficult to approach Him.

Most People Relate to God Based on Their Works and Sins

Sad as it is, I have discovered that most people in the world, as well as people in church, relate to God based on their works and sins. As hard as it was for John to grasp God's love, it is just as difficult for thousands of people—even in church—to understand the dimensions of the love of God. In my mind's eye, I can see God trying His best to explain who He really is to His children. I can see nervous smiles on the faces of millions, as their hearts say yes but the cognitive mind, with its critical reasoning, puts God's love in categories such as impossible or make believe.

How can we ever understand God, know who He is, and relate to Him in a world that perceives Him to be something quite abnormal? John would not have minded sitting next to a police officer, rocket scientist, doctor or even a politician. He could even have a fearless and interesting conversation with a pilot or a schoolteacher, with no problem. Yet, he was very uncomfortable with me because his heart believes God is angry and disappointed with Him.

Fear, based on lies told about God, holds us back from being at ease in our relationship with God.

As human beings, we all have certain things in common. There is a kind of *common sense*, which gives us a point of reference from where we communicate and learn to know each other. We are all human, we all need a place to stay, and we all work for a living. We are all relationship-oriented beings with the need to love and be loved, and we all need security and a hope for the future. It is within this undefined yet common logic that we relate to one another. We reason and relate inside the *logic of our design.*

A picture about God that is alien to normal family life has

been painted about God, resulting in pain and fear in the lives of millions of people.

Let's say you find yourself seated next to an alien from outer space on your next flight. You won't have a clue what to say! Since you know nothing about what kind of being it is, you will have no idea whether it can even understand your language or culture. Imagine how frightened you would feel, approaching an alien, if all you've ever heard about them is that they're violent and want to kill people. If we're convinced that aliens are extra-terrestrial beings, who know our very thoughts but consider us their enemies, we will find it almost impossible to relate to them. Sadly, this is the picture that has been painted about God, causing great fear in the hearts of people.

In attempting to communicate with an alien, all our questions would be relationship-based and in line with *our* logic, the only means by which we could attempt to make sense of the alien. Since our concerns would naturally lean towards such things as morality, family life, safety and survival, we would be limited in our ability to define a creature that does not relate to any aspects of our logic. So, unless we are the same kind of beings, with the same logic and needs, we will never be able to fully comprehend each other or relate in a meaningful way. Aliens cannot function inside the parameters of being human, so we would feel quite distant and uncomfortable with them.

We relate to people based on similar life experiences and shared ground, so that when we perceive others as different, we tend to veer away from them while we are naturally drawn to people with whom we can more comfortably relate. When I am in another country and hear someone speaking Afrikaans, I am not afraid to walk up to him and start a conversation. What gives me this boldness is the fact that we share the same culture and language, and we have the same country of origin.

If God is seen as a dangerous alien, you will never be comfortable with Him next to you. In order to have a meaningful relationship with God we need to find common ground or our hearts will keep Him at a distance.

What do we share in common with God?

As we consider this, the following questions beg to be answered:

God is a being who needs nothing and no one. He lives as I AM that I AM. How could I ever understand Him?

Does not His very being, as God, place a demand on me to change into something else?

How could I not feel intimidated?

How can we relate to God, based on our design as relationship-oriented beings?

If we don't really know God, we do feel intimidated and wonder if we must change to be in relationship with Him. Like the gentlemen sitting next to me on my flights, the mere thought of God can trigger feelings of guilt and fear, even anger. We instinctively feel we must please a being with whom we cannot relate. After all, God created the universe—He's way out of our league! What pressure, trying to please the One with whom we cannot relate! At best, we will have a shallow relationship—like that of a human and animal relationship. Let me explain what I mean by likening this to the "relationship" I have with my dog.

Our dog is black and white, so we named him Piano. I can see that he loves me from the depth of his being; he is 100 percent loyal and committed to me. He obeys me with great enthusiasm and would never do anything to harm me. In fact, I believe he would give his life for me. However, thcrc is onc thing I need that he falls short in, and that is intimate fellowship. I need someone with whom I can share my deepest feelings, but Piano doesn't really understand me. As much as I love him, I cannot communicate with him like I do with someone close to me, like Helena or my sons. The reason for this is obvious; we are not of the same kind. While I am a human being, he is the dog kind of animal being.

For Us to Have a Meaningful Relationship with God, He Has to Be as Much Our Kind as We are His

No amount of loyalty and obedience, or adoration and worship, my dog Piano bestows on me can ever be enough to form a truly meaningful relationship. He will never know what it is to be like me. It is impossible for him to enter my life and share it with me like another human being can. He cannot appreciate a good theological book, nor can he understand a profound movie or enjoy a beautiful show at the opera house. All he can do is adore me, but he can never share in my quality of life. We are actually worlds apart. No amount of food I give him, or love and respect I show him, will ever enable him to experience, for example, the emotions I feel when one of my sons wins a tennis match or gets 100 percent on a test at school. Our pets can never relate with us the way we human beings relate with one another.

Throughout my life, I have discovered that people often relate to God as a dog relates to its master. When people are happy to see their Master and want to obey Him, they go to great lengths to prove their loyalty to Him. They think that by obeying the rules they will earn God's approval and provision. When they feel they have failed to keep up the necessary good works, they run and hide from God. This is truly a sad way to live.

Piano's "good works," like displaying joy when he sees me, protecting me, even just being in my presence, as well as his obedience to my commands, can never cause him to enter my level of life. Even *my* loyal provision for *him* cannot elevate him to what I am. He can sleep on my couch, or even sleep in a golden dog box and eat steak every day, but he is stuck in being dog.

God never intended for us to obey commands so that we could earn His daily provisions. What He wants for us is to share His quality of life. How sad it would be if we were to fall into such deep darkness that we would define ourselves by—and find our existence in—how much God gives us! The truth is, we can only find our identity and value in knowing Him and knowing ourselves as He has always known us, never in our obedience and the amount of money He is willing to give us!

Unless we recognize that we are truly 100 percent God's

kind, we will never be able to have a meaningful relationship with Him or share in His quality of life. We will not know how to relate to Him; we will be nervous and won't know what to do in His presence. The quickest way to kill a relationship is for people to be confused about who they truly are; that's when side issues like money, health and all other provision-related matters take centre stage.

Believing the foundation of a relationship is obedience to all kinds of principles is a total misunderstanding of the true meaning of relationship. Furthermore, falling in love with the prosperity that might be the outcome of obedience to principles will surely be the death of the relationship. In **GOD** we live and move and have our being, so we relate to God within the reality that we are the God-kind, and not in what we can do for Him or how He can bless us in this life!

Seeing that it is not possible to have a meaningful relationship with God when we have a wrong idea of who He really is, let us see if we can find out who He really is. I have heard it being said that you can know who a person really is when you know what he is like when he is alone

The God before Time

When I consider that God is love and has always been love, the following questions arise:

- *If God has always been alone, whom did He love and how did He express love before time?*
- *If God is grace (which, in the Greek, means to influence unto the manifestation of true life), on whom*

did He bestow His grace, or influence, before time?
- *If God is kind, to whom did He show His kindness before time?*

The Name of God

Previously, I always thought of God as a lonely god and pictured Him as a kind of super holy being somewhere in outer space. I envisioned Him as a bright light in dark outer space, just floating in nothingness, staring straight ahead, and living in solitude. The words I would use to describe Him would be *monotone*, *distant*, *lonely*, *holy*, *scary*, *a bright light*, *alone*, *cold*, *unfriendly*—everything but human. To summarize, I would have said that God is indescribably alone, distant and unreachable. Imagine how difficult it would be to relate to such a being. It would certainly be impossible!

I have found that a revelation of how loving and caring God is in the Trinity, even before time, deepens my understanding of Him being only good. The picture of a God who has always been happy and full of joy helps my heart to rest in the fact that He is good in the depth of His being. It is almost like spying on God when He is alone and realizing that the good He shows is not a smoke screen; it is genuine.

Let's see what the Bible says about God before time:

*"In the beginning **God** created the heaven and the earth" (NKJV, Gen.1:1).*

In a Jewish setting, a person's name speaks about who and what he is. A good example of this would be the name

Jesus. Scripture states that the angel told Joseph to name the baby *Jesus*, which means *Saviour*, for He would save His people from their sins. Thus, in essence, the person of Jesus is described by His name. With this truth in mind, we can have a look at the word *Elohim (Eloheem),* which translated to English is **God**.

Look at the word *God* in the Hebrew language:

"In the beginning ***God***$^{\textbf{\textit{H430}}}$ *created the heaven and the earth" (KJV, Gen. 1:1).*

"And ***God***$^{\textbf{\textit{H430}}}$ *said, Let Us make man in our image, after our likeness;" (KJV, Gen. 1:26a).*

Strong's Hebrew/English dictionary

H430 *el-o-heem'* **Plural** of H433; *gods* in the ordinary sense;

(H433, which is NOT the Hebrew word in Genesis 1:1 and 1:26, translates as *el-o'-ah,el-o'-ah - a deity* or the *deity*: - God, **singular**)

The word *El-o'ah* (H433), by itself, is the word for *God.* This singular word does not say much; it says no more to me than the concept of a monotone, distant, impersonal God, like I described earlier. The singular form does not imply relationship at all. On the other hand, *Elohim*(H430), which is in both verses above, is the **plural** for *God* (H433) from where we can extrapolate a lot of information.

If God is one, and yet also more than one, it implies

wonderful unity and union between more than one being. This speaks of relationship, ongoing communication and many other key relational values. According to this definition, we can use the phrase *Divine Ones* (*H430 BDB),* instead of *God*, when we read Gen.1:1. (I prefer to say *Divine Ones*, rather than *gods*, since the word *gods* commonly refers to false gods.) The verse could actually read: "In the beginning *the Divine Ones* created the heaven and the earth" (Gen. 1:1).

I can still remember how amazed I was the first time I saw this. As a preacher, it shocks you in two ways: first, if it is contrary to what you have believed, it forces you to start thinking outside the box. Secondly, you see a truth that could have you labelled as a heretic, if you preach it. When I first read this, it felt as if the ground fell away beneath me. How could this be! Is God not One as the Scripture states? Is there not just one God?

Yes, God is One

The Bible declares that God is **one** in Deut. 6:4:

"Hear, O Israel: The LORD our God is ***one*** *LORD" (KJV).*

"Hear, O Israel: The LORD our God, the LORD is ***one****" (ESV).*

I believe Deuteronomy 6:4 accurately describes God. I would translate that verse to say:

Listen with understanding, and see O Israel, that the Self-existing One (Jehovah), our Trinity of Divine Ones

(Elohim), are in perfect oneness (That is to say, unity) (Bertie Brits).

We also see this concept in Genesis 11:6, where the people who built the Tower of Babel were described as being "one." It does not mean that only one man built the tower, but that the thousands who were building it were in **perfect unison**:

And the LORD said, Behold, the people is one, and they have all one language; and this they begin to do: and now will be restrained from them, which they have imagined to do (KJV, Gen. 11:6).

AND God is more than One

The moment the concept of *Divine OneS* enters our reasoning, it opens a brand new understanding of God. When you read, *Divine OneS* (**plural**), instead of *Divine One (*singular), several questions come to mind:

How do these beings relate?
Are there more references that confirm the plural concept?
What makes them divine?
How do we define divinity?
Do they have different personalities?

Who are the Divine Ones?

The answer is simple: **Father, Son** and **Holy Spirit**.

Look at that description of the **Trinity**! It is flooded with God's family logic, which always sounds like the loving

Dad that He is, who deeply cherishes His family: "I am your Father, you are my Son, and you, our dear Holy Spirit, are also One with us in this family. I can't but love you with everything I am, for we are One!" The Son talked often about His Trinity family, like in John 20:17 when He had risen and appeared to Mary Magdalene. Notice He also includes **us** in His family:

Jesus said to her, "Do not cling to Me, for I have not yet ascended to My Father; but go to My brethren and say to them, 'I am ascending to My Father and your Father, and to My God and your God.'" (*NKJV*, John 20:17).

Do you see the family relationships in that verse, and how we are also included? We are Jesus' **brethren**, or brothers (and sisters, ladies), and God is not only Jesus' Father, but also *our* Father! We are family!

Genesis 1:26 and 27 is one of the Scriptures that reveal the most to me, concerning the pre-creation state of the Divine Ones:

26*And God said, Let Us make man in our image, after our*
likeness: and let them have dominion over the fish of the
sea, and over the fowl of the air, and over the cattle, and
over all the earth, and over every creeping thing that
creepeth upon the earth. 27*So God created man in his*
(own) image, in the image of God created He him; male
and female created He them (*KJV*, Gen.1:26, 27).

It would be entirely correct to translate the above Scriptures: "And the Divine One**s** said, let's make man in **our** image and likeness."

The moment we look at the verse with this truth in mind, new revelation life flows from it. First, the words *let us*, (or let's), reveal a lot about the Divine Ones. Something is revealed that we, as humans, are acquainted with—something that is part of *our* design as human beings. *Let's* implies relationship between equals who honour and love each other. It's as if one asks the other permission to do something, in a mutually considerate relationship between equals. Saying, "let's," shows humility, a heart for unity, and even the desire to not exclude the thought and positive input of the other. It implies unity and love. We can understand even more about the Divine Ones by looking at what the one requested of the others: "Let us (let's) make man in our image and likeness …"

When I read this verse, I can see myself sitting around the table with my family whom I dearly love. I see us playing a board game, laughing, making jokes and having great fun. As an idea comes to mind that can benefit us all, I say, "Let's go to Cape Town tomorrow and spend our day on Table Mountain." The "let's" is not a command, but rather like asking permission or making a suggestion to people who are already fulfilled and enjoying themselves. "Let's" shows the respect I have for my family, in humbly submitting my idea to them, while acknowledging their free choice. It shows that **I regard them as my equals**. You could phrase the *let's* as the question, "Would it be alright with you, if we go down to Cape Town and spend the day on Table Mountain?"

The question carries with it the expectation or foreknowledge that of course they would consent. Therefore, the suggestion is phrased as a rhetorical question. I believe it would not be wrong to translate

Genesis1:26 as, "Would it be alright with you two if, together, we make a being called *man* into our image and likeness, and give him a seat with us at our table?" This is asked with a clear expectation, or foreknowledge, that there will be consensus about it. Although it still does not fully explain the interaction in Genesis 1:26, an example that is much closer to what happened in the Trinity would be the following:

Imagine a happily married couple sitting at a table and the husband says, "Wouldn't' it be nice if we had a baby? Then we would have someone like us, sitting here next to us, with whom we can share our life." This kind of rhetorical question reveals their closeness to each other, and their unity in mind and emotion.

We can conclude, by looking at Genesis1:26, that the Divine Ones are relationally oriented beings, intimately interacting with each other, who co-existed even before the creation of the world. We can also conclude that they honour each other and live in such a way that the others' opinions and freewill are respected and taken into consideration. We can see that these Divine Ones are not threatened by having others sharing in their nature—their very being. We see they are generously sharing their lives. We can also understand the **mind-set** in which the Divine Ones created man, Heaven, Earth and all that is in it.

God is Someone Designed Just like Me

As I studied these Scriptures and understood more about God's being, I realized that my perception of Him changed from being distant—even alien to mankind—to someone who can be described in human terms. He is someone with whom I can relate from the core of my being, designed just like me.

Reading Genesis 1:27 again, I concluded that we can understand the being of God, the Divine Ones by looking at humans who are made in their very image and likeness:

So God (the Divine Ones) created man in his (their) own image, in the image of the Divine Ones created He him; male and female created He them (*ISV*, Gen.1:27).

I love the way Genesis 1:27 is written. First of all, we see that God (the Divine *Ones* - **plural**) created a *man* (**singular**), in His image and in His likeness "created He *him* (**singular**); male and female created He *them* (**plural**)." Here we can clearly see that a human could never be in the likeness and image of God, if he were alone. God Himself said that it is not good for man to be alone, but why?

It is not good for a human being to be alone because solitude is not an environment in which one can express his or her being, having all the ability but nowhere to manifest it. This is true because a human is a relational being that originated from the Divine Ones and all that is God. The Scripture states that we live, move, and have our being in God.

If a human is a being God has **designed** for communication, with whom will he talk? If God made a human as a being capable of giving and receiving love, whom will he love? If trust is in his design, whom shall he trust? If God made him to be kind and receive kindness, with whom will he be kind? If his nature is to help, whom will he help? If he is influential, whom will he influence? If God created him to procreate, to whom will he say, "Let's have someone of our own kind"? And then who will answer, "Yes, let's"?

We see that God made mankind male *and* female, demonstrating how God is a relational being, who put man in a healthy male and female relationship, thus reflecting Himself. We are relational beings who function from the foundation of love. God made humans to function inside the parameters of love, expressed in belief, faith, trust, joy, peace, respect, understanding, knowing, openness, mutual influence, freedom of choice and kindness.

Our *design* functions optimally in the atmosphere of security, which is found in love and mutual respect. God gave man the opportunity to feel how it feels to be like Him, having the life that expresses itself in these wonderful ways, with love as its source. Since we are in the image and likeness of God, it would be impossible for us to have any meaningful relationship outside of these parameters, for we experience life inside them. Trying to live on any other basis than that of our design would be fatal. We should base our theological doctrine on this foundation; anything outside it would be false and distance our hearts from God.

As I was meditating on the relationship between the Divine Ones, in whom we have our being, I asked God to help me define this reality in simple terms. What I felt the Lord say to me was that He is our Father, our Husband and our Friend, and that we are His children, bride and friends. I believe I was inspired by the Holy Spirit as I asked myself what God is actually saying when He declares Himself our Father, Husband and Friend? Then I realized He was saying that we are His family, and that we live and have our being inside the reality in which He lives, which is a **family** reality. *Family life* is the best way to describe the relational dynamics between the Divine Ones. Anything other than family realities would be outside the life God lives.

When I read, in Genesis, that God came "in the cool of the day" to speak to Adam, I see relationship written all over it. What was true in Heaven became true on Earth! Humankind is now partaking of the life possessed in the Godhead. As it is in Heaven, so it is on Earth! God wanted Adam to function exactly like Him and made sure that we would be able to understand that today. Let's have a look at Adam giving the animals names. In Genesis 2:18-23, we can clearly see how Adam functioned:

18GOD said, It is not good for the Man to be alone; I'll make him a helper, a companion. 19So GOD formed from the dirt of the ground all the animals of the field and all the birds of the air. He brought them to the Man to see what he would name them. Whatever the Man called each living creature that was its name. 20The Man named the cattle, named the birds of the air, named the wild animals; but he did not find a suitable companion. 21GOD put the Man into a deep sleep. As he slept he removed one of his ribs and replaced it with flesh. 22GOD then used the rib that he had taken from the Man to make Woman and presented her to the Man. 23The Man said, "Finally! Bone of my bone, flesh of my flesh! Name her Woman for she was made from Man" (*KJV*, Gen.2:18-23).

Adam named the animals and concluded that there was no one in creation like him. A name of something spells its nature, and as Adam named them, he could not find any creature that was like him. Then God brought forth Eve from Adam's rib and presented her to him. Right away Adam recognized his own kind!

Because Adam was in the image and likeness of God, he could never have had a companion from the animal kingdom. It's as if this event is telling us how Adam had a desire to have fellowship with his own kind, and to see fruit coming forth from that relationship. Adam needed family. God was Adam's kind, but the God-kind-in-human- flesh (Adam) was alone on Earth. By bringing Eve for Adam, God gave expression to the reality in the Godhead; together, Adam and Eve expressed His image and likeness. Or, another way of saying it, God needed an Adam and an Eve to manifest His image and likeness on the earth, not just an Adam.

All these things speak of having a love-based relationship inside a unity called *family*. It's amazing that Adam could not produce fruit (express himself), until he could behold himself in another. He could only become one with another being that would fit his being. When he had flesh of his flesh and bone of his bone (See Gen. 2:23), with whom he could share his life, Adam could really begin to live the life God intended for him, bearing fruit after his own kind and rooted in love. When Eve came forth, the Divine Ones (God) saw that their life was alive in humans and fully represented in humans, then He said it was VERY good (See Gen. 1:31).

There is a Person in the Trinity who is Human Flesh

and Bone, Representing all of Humanity. We are in the God-family.

For human beings to have the life that God has, they need to see themselves in God. How could that be made possible? It could only be possible if there was a human in the Trinity, and there is one! His name is Jesus! Because of Jesus, the same reality in which Adam and Eve existed with God exists now between God and us. There is a person in the Trinity who is human flesh and bone, representing all of humanity.

The family logic, or *common sense* of God, is the foundation of the relationship we have with Him. Whenever we reason outside *family logic,* we reason outside the borders of His being and ours. Living in realities outside *family reality is* unnatural for humankind and will ultimately lead to destruction for all those who choose to do so. There is still much more to say about the Divine Ones' family logic, but what I have explained will suffice for the purpose of this book.

As we continue to talk about money, we need to keep to this simple truth as our logic and reasoning. Otherwise, we will move into the area of darkness and death in our doctrine. All Scripture is God-inspired and finds its origin in the logic of God. All Scripture is inspired by the Trinity and has to convey their very nature. With this logic of the Trinity in mind, I'd like to share my personal journey with you.existed with God exists now between God and us. There is a person in the Trinity who is human flesh and bone, representing all of humanity.

The family logic, or *common sense* of God, is the

foundation of the relationship we have with Him. Whenever we reason outside *family logic,* we reason outside the borders of His being and ours. Living in realities outside *family reality is* unnatural for humankind and will ultimately lead to destruction for all those who choose to do so. There is still much more to say about the Divine Ones' family logic, but what I have explained will suffice for the purpose of this book.

As we continue to talk about money, we need to keep to this simple truth as our logic and reasoning. Otherwise, we will move into the area of darkness and death in our doctrine. All Scripture is God-inspired and finds its origin in the logic of God. All Scripture is inspired by the Trinity and has to convey their very nature. With this logic of the Trinity in mind, I'd like to share my personal journey with you.

CHAPTER 2

The Death of My ABBA

Imagine a money-free world. Imagine a life free of lack, where all people have whatever they need and in abundance. Most people would describe this as Heaven. One could almost connect all problems in the world to money in one way or another. If it wasn't for money, we would not have the drug trade, blood diamonds, corruption, wars, pride, political fights, church splits - the list goes on and on. I'm sure I could fill a 200-page book with examples of the evil that is in the world, presumably because of money.

I can still remember the first time I read the verse that I thought stated, "Money is the root of all evil." Confusion grabbed my heart, when I read this in 1Timothy 6:10, because I knew that money is what we need to survive in this world: *Who can live without this "evil" thing called money?* I could not imagine the church living a money-free life, so it seemed to me that we were forced to live with something that was actually evil. My next thought summarized all I knew at the time: *If I just don't desire a lot of money I will be fairly safe.* Then, about two years later, my understanding of 1Timothy 6:10 was "corrected," while I was listening to a televangelist. He pointed out that Scripture does not say *money* is the root of evil; it says the *love of* money is the root of evil. He also clarified that we should not be worried about having money, for money is neither good nor bad. However, he warned us that money does reveal that which is in the heart of a man. I was amazed to hear this "prosperity gospel" that sounded so wonderful. It was saying that Jesus died so that I could be a millionaire—even a billionaire! It also taught me that a good person would use money to save lives and provide for others, while a bad one would use it in a way that manifests the evil in his heart. Such joy flooded my heart when I was liberated from thinking that money is evil!

After listening to many preachers, my thinking changed and I agreed with the belief that "Jesus paid for people to be rich." My renewed thoughts felt like such a relief, compared to my previous fears about money: *If I don't desire riches, I am actually against what He came to freely give me.* This "revelation" felt like a kind of healing of my mind, freeing me from the belief and frustration of thinking money is evil: *If Jesus wants to heal me from poverty and make me a billionaire who am I to argue! I should be a millionaire! Refusing to be rich is like refusing to be healed; I'd be dishonouring the cross!*

The prosperity gospel had convinced me that it would be disrespectful if I did not want to become extremely rich: *After all, Jesus died so that I could have wealth; thus, salvation can only be defined by an abundance of money and material possessions.* I now know that when people believe this about money, they are unable to be saved from the power money has over their lives. When money is the loudest voice one hears, the only "salvation" available is to find ways to make more money. In obedience to what I thought was the truth, I opened up my heart for prosperity. In the same way that I was open to healing and loved it, I started to love prosperity. I loved the fact that the curse of poverty was broken so that I could be rich—and really *should* be rich! Not that I saw myself as poor up until then; in fact, I was never even aware that I was poor. I always thought that I was blessed, until it dawned on me that I was actually poor and just didn't know it. My eyes were opened to see my "nakedness and poverty," as they put it, and I was a bit ashamed.

I Desired Riches as Passionately as I Desired to Preach

I was determined not to disappoint God, so I started desiring riches and affluence just as I had always desired to preach. I would do everything possible to see that it happened because I did not want to be disrespectful, in any way, to what Jesus had done for me. If He died for me to be rich, I was going to be as rich as possible. I was going to be just as rich as He could make me! I knew that if I did my part, He would do His. I loved the expectation of becoming rich, as it was "God's dream" for me. I was sure my blessing was just around the corner and that I was on the brink of a massive breakthrough: *This will be my year of increase and multiplication,* I thought, *It will be the year when all that the locusts have destroyed will be returned to me sevenfold* (See Joel 2:25, Prov. 6:31).

The time of contentment was over, as many preachers would say, "To be happy with where you are, and what you have, is selfish! Not moving on to greater things and bigger financial visions, means that you are backslidden and selfish." I was persuaded that being happy with what I had was a slap in the face of God, as well as a bad example to the world. Who would ever believe the word of a poor man? I started dreaming, and I dreamed big, very big: *Well, God wants me to be rich, doesn't He? So, I will have all that I'm dreaming of and more!*

I Could Hear the Voice of Financial Supply so Clearly!

I began to get a vision from God for the money I was about to receive from Him. It was as if God was showing me masses of unsaved people, so that the burning in my heart for the individual was multiplied a billion times. It was not about the one lost sheep anymore: *We will go big now— big stages, big auditoriums, and, and ...* Visions and strategies started coming to me "supernaturally," almost as if a new life from God was born inside me. I could hear the voice of financial supply so clearly!

This new revelation about money also changed how I felt about others. I felt greater and greater respect for the Christians who "had it made," financially. Previously, I was not aware of whether somebody was rich or poor, never even noticing what vehicle a person drove or where he stayed. All I saw was the person, unconcerned about whether or not they were "financially blessed." But, after my newfound belief of financial prosperity, I realized that I used to be a bit arrogant back in the day when it didn't matter to me where I came from socially or how much money I had. I just believed that I would always have enough to give and to be of use. Now I saw how arrogant I was back then: W*ho was I to think that I could teach rich*

Christians about God!

Furthermore, through this seemingly amazing message that "God wants you to be rich, for riches are a manifestation of godliness," I believed God was enlightening me to the way He blessed people with material possessions. I thought, *those wealthy Christians must be doing everything right to be so close to God and to have such a special 'revelation.'* Feeling more welcome in church and understanding the "church world" a bit better, I was finally seeing what everything was really about: *We faithful Christians are waiting for the "wealth of the wicked," which is actually intended for us!*

As time went by and I saw no financial blessing in my life, I wanted the affirmation of being rich even more. But, no matter how often I confessed slogans like "money cometh," money did not "cometh" to me! I desperately longed to please God by being rich. In fact, I longed to be so rich that even a Jew would become jealous of me. Then I could point him to Jesus and lead him to walk in the fullness of the cross. Instead, the more I craved money, the more I found guilt slowly flooding my heart. I was ashamed I did not have the money some of my friends had and to drive the car I drove. All of a sudden, the old car that I first saw as a blessing became a curse, a blatant sign of my weak faith, and even worse, an indication of some hidden disobedience or misapplication of a principle somewhere in my life. Something had to be wrong; I felt I needed advice.

Jesus Did It All and the Tithe Unleashed It All?

I was desperate for answers and the answers came through

a well-known preacher who visited our church to preach on money. He had it all—the big ministry, the jet, and the missing link between my money and me. The preacher introduced me to the "**tithe**," as one of the keys to the system on which God's provision functions: *Oh, hallelujah! Freedom at last! Let me first pay God what is His, and then all that Jesus died for will start to manifest in my life!* It all sounded so simple: Jesus did it all and the tithe unleashed it all. I was beginning to understand that although God does love the generosity of my giving to various needs in the moment, He is a God of order and needs my giving to be in line with His **system**: First we have to tithe, for the tithe is what we "owe God."

I became persuaded that I was wrongly giving away money, by giving as it pleased me, money that was not even mine in the first place! Thus, I was actually stealing from God. I was randomly giving away the money that should have gone to the local church for people in need—albeit lovingly—but through my own will.

I Stole from God by Giving to the Poor and Preaching to the Lost

When I asked God to forgive me for giving money to the wrong people, I felt the burden of guilt leave me. The guilt for being poor also lifted, in the brightness of my expectation of a new financial life. Everything was about to change; I felt the joy of a new found belief, the joy of a new beginning: *How could I have ever thought that God could bless me when I was actually stealing from Him? Even if my heart was pure and sincere in helping the poor and spreading the Gospel with the means I had, it was wrong—sincerely wrong!* God loved me enough to chastise me, revealing the truth. It was painful to think that I stole from God by autonomously giving to the poor and preaching to the lost with His money.

When I realized the tithe is the foundation of financial provision, I knew that even if God loved me and wanted to bless me, He couldn't: *How could He bless a thief who robbed Heaven!* I was convinced I was that **thief** and that I was **cursed** for robbing God. My poverty (which I was unaware of prior to learning that God wanted me to be rich) was, in fact, a direct result of my disobedience. When I found out that I was guilty of robbing God, I was so grateful that I could come to the right knowledge in order to change for the better.

To correct the wrong I had done, I decided to give to the church the money I had always given to the poor and spent on outreach. I had no fear in doing this, because I believed my breakthrough would happen before the end of the following month. Surely then I would lack nothing: *Did God not clearly say that I could prove and test Him on this specific point?* I understood that you could never test God, except in the matter of the tithe:

Bring ye all the tithes into the storehouse, that there may be meat in mine house, and prove me now herewith, saith the LORD of hosts, if I will not open you the windows of heaven, and pour you out a blessing, that there shall not be room enough to receive it (*KJV*, Mal. 3:10).

The Almighty cannot lie; therefore, I will have a lot of money and be super-blessed not long from now! The God who saved me, the One who gave me His Holy Spirit, and gave His Son for me will not fail me. I failed Him because

I used His money for outreach and the poor, independent of church authority!

I was actually astonished that I could live a Christian life, leading people to Jesus, and even seeing miracles, without being aware of one of the greatest truths in the church called the *tithe!* Obviously, the tithe is vitally important to blessedness in a Christian's life, as it is preached every Sunday for at least the first ten or fifteen minutes of the service.

I was amazed to see God in a new light now, as a loving *and* "righteous" God; take note—not just loving, but loving *and righteous*. Suddenly, I saw something new about Him: God could curse you if you stole from Him! I was never even aware that God could curse someone, prior to this new understanding. I felt that I had matured as a believer because I was getting to know "the other side of God." And all of this was revealed to me in one small truth: "**Financial blessedness shows godliness**."

I must say, I did not steal a lot from God. When I realized my error, I began to give God what He wanted: *His 10 percent is now with Him. Of the leftover money, I will give to the poor and pay for fuel to preach to the lost.* I was not a thief anymore.

It Was as if I Entered a Curse

The first month came and went without the breakthrough. I can remember not having a cent leftover two days before the end of the month. Nevertheless, I just knew the miracle would happen in the last two days because I still had bills to pay. *God is not a liar, after all.* That month came and went. Likewise, the second month came and went without any breakthrough. In fact, I was worse off than ever before. I had no money to give to the poor and had to cycle to my outreach project at night, which was in a very dangerous area. I did not have fuel for my old car, which proved my poverty. It was as if I had entered a curse, like someone had cast a spell over me. It was the complete opposite of what I expected. In those two months, I found that my compassion for the poor was fading, as I was beginning to think their poverty was their own fault: *If they tithed as I do, and stopped stealing from God, they would be much better off.* I concluded that I had no obligation towards them, for their poverty was the fruit of their own disobedience. I also thought I could sense God's anger at those who did not want to give to me. Convinced they were in rebellion for not giving me money, I felt I had an inner witness that God would deal with them according to their rebellion: *They would rather live extravagantly, buying nice houses and the newest cars, while I tithe and don't even have enough food on the table.*

My heart slowly started to change. The innocent child who loved all people, and lived freely and happily while loving God, had now grown into "maturity," understanding the "deeper things of God." I was surely moving into a big ministry—so I thought—just as soon as I received the money that would manifest because of my tithe. I would soon be a "mover and shaker," who would "conquer the world for Jesus!"

Something else happened in me after my new found belief about the tithe. To me, the tithe doctrine was not simply about giving a tithe. As people, we learn who a person really is by looking at his actions and lifestyle; thus, the tithe teaching brought me to a place where I thought I was beginning to better understand the person of God, as a new picture of Him was forming in my mind.

I also came to believe that the Gospel is not as simple as I thought it was. Although I had always seen God as my loving Father, who loves and blesses me unconditionally, my views on His provision changed after accepting the tithe teaching. I learned unconditional provision is only a kind of starting place: *The God I am dealing with now values affluence and wants me to have more. Therefore, as He gives me the ability to gain wealth, I will enter the blessed place of being "in His perfect will."*

I knew I could do it; God and I could conquer the world! I believed He had given me the ability and the means to do my part, so that I could become as He is. All I needed to do was to give 10 percent of the money He would give me. I thought that was well within my ability. Besides, I loved Him enough to do it.

This is how what I perceived to be the "righteous side" of God was born in me. I began to see people for what I thought they truly were, now that I comprehended the "bigger picture." Previously, I had only a one-sided view of people, but now I also saw them from the "righteous side" of God, and began to understand why they were going through hard times. My "eyes of justice and righteousness" were opened to see that since God did His part to save and bless us, so that we could become rich, we must now do our part. Now that I could truly define people by how they did their part, it was easy for me to direct them towards having life, and life in abundance. All I needed to do to help them out of their distress was to point out their shortcomings and all would be fine—IF they obeyed.

All Depended on Me

I was excited to learn more of what I could do to make things work for me. God did His part and all depended on me now. I could never have imagined what a big change understanding a simple principle could bring to my life. My view of God changed from Him being my Abba to Him as Lord, Ruler, Master and Leader of the Battle. The view I had of myself also changed; I still saw myself as His son, but now also as His "servant."

In my pursuit of all He intended for me to be and have, **I employed my willpower** in order to have the "more" He intended. I began to read the Bible from the perspective of finding more keys to the life He wanted for me: *If I have a part in obtaining money, I must have a part in other things, as well*. These thoughts were not only born from my cognitive decision-making, but also through conception in my subconscious mind. The teaching I received on money changed my belief about who God is and how His kingdom functions.

I Longed for the Days When I Felt Holy and Loved

Months later, seeing no financial prosperity and feeling negative and slightly depressed, all I could conclude was that there was something wrong with *me*. Every now and then, I would reminisce about the days when I just preached freely—when I did not have the "big vision." In my inner man, I longed for those days when I felt holy and loved. In those days, things came easily to me; God opened doors and I was not money-conscious at all.

For a time, I lived in the bliss of ignorance … the good old days. When I thought about these things, I felt a sense of guilt and an unwillingness to "mature." I would tell God that the maturing thing was hard for me, but I was willing to submit and change into the man He wanted me to be… and so I tithed. Yet, I did not see any financial increase in my life. I knew it was *my* fault, for God could not make a mistake: *Did He not call me, give me the desire to preach, and grant me large visions and a principle by which I could obtain the financial means to get it done?*

I followed the principle but it did not seem to work; I needed answers. Yet, I would never have said, "Tithing does not work," for then I would be declaring God a liar and I knew He was not. So, I went to the local pastor for advice and even for correction if that was what I needed. When he told me that the prosperity preacher who taught on money would be back at his church the next Sunday, I was so happy. I knew that preacher had it all working for him; certainly, he could help me to have it all, too!

The next week, in listening to what the man was preaching, I realized my mistake. I had been tithing but never sowed seed! *How could I have missed it, when the Bible states it plainly!* This was when I came to understand the wonderfully liberating truth of "sowing and reaping." It works like this: First of all, the tithe belongs to God; then once the tithe is given, it activates the sowing principle. God would see whatever I gave on top of 10 percent as *seed*. This is how God would see your faith and how you activated your own faith. "Multiplication comes in hundredfold, sixty-fold and thirtyfold," the preacher explained. He also said that we should not push our expectation too far, at first, but to start with expecting only tenfold for the first month.

The first thing I did, after hearing that message, was to repent for not sowing. Did I not know that millions of people could be lost if I couldn't get this principle to work! *This time it has to work. I need to save people, and I need to get in line with the perfect will of God for me, which is to be rich.* Then, I started giving 33 percent of my income to the local church. The preacher made it very clear that you should sow into "good soil," not just anywhere. You might mess it all up by sowing into soil that is not fertile. It was also emphasized that the best soil is always the most successful ministry, which in this case, was our local church or the preacher himself.

This stopped all my voluntary giving. I gave 33 percent of my income to the church and paid my bible school fees with the rest. I had no money left, not even money for food. But I had a great hope, for surely the sowing-and-reaping principle would *work*. When the preacher shared testimony after testimony of how it worked for many people, I thought, *God loves me and it will also work for me.*

After one month, nothing happened. I spoke to the local pastor and he told me to walk by faith, trusting the breakthrough was at the door, and to not give up hope. Helena (my girlfriend at the time) worked at a local restaurant and told me that I could eat there once a day, as she would share her food with me. She stole from the restaurant's surplus food, thus keeping me alive, since the sowing and tithing principle had not kicked in yet for me. I had nothing but the hope that it would work.

The Voice and Embrace of My Loving Father was Gone

As all this was happening, I started thinking that *I must have hidden sin.* I felt like shouting out to God, "My Abba, my Abba, where are you!"

The voice of the Righteous god was always there, the voice of the Ruler was there, the voice of the Battle leader was loud and clear, the voice of the Precept god thundered, but the voice of my Abba was only a memory. My Abba had become Precept god, Obedience god, Righteousness god, Tithe god, Ruler god, and Kingdom god. The voice and embrace of my loving Abba was something I longed for, but it was gone.

I had entered the world of "mature Christians," and was a bit scared. Like a small child, I wanted to cry out for my Daddy to help me, but the **Precept god** would quickly correct me, saying, "Remember, I am a god of order and principles. As long as the earth remains, sowing time and harvest time will remain. The sooner you get this to work, the better. I know you can. Let's do it."

The **Righteous god** would say, "Please make sure that you don't kill the seed. Live right. You don't want to sin while the seed is in the ground, for it will die that way."

The **Ruler god** said, "I am glad you took dominion over poverty by giving so much. Keep it up; we need to conquer the world."

The **Tithe god** said, "Well done! Keep giving your 10 percent. If you stop, all the seed will be wasted and you will reap nothing!"

The **Obedience god** would say, "Keep being obedient in all these things, for the lives of people depend on it. Don't question the Scriptures or leadership, for rebellion is like witchcraft." That second month, I felt that I was giving my best. I was keeping it up; I would obey, I would win, and God and I would make this work. I would not fail Him. In this desperate time, while I was open to anything that could help me, I was introduced to the submission-and-covering message, the spiritual-warfare-anoint-everything message, the spiritual-mapping message, the prayer-and-fasting-for- more-anointing message … the list goes on. I tried to follow all of these to the letter, while winning souls and attending bible school. Yet, doing all these things did not bring the breakthrough.

In desperation, I went to another pastor in the church to share my situation with him. After carefully listening, he told me that he just had an "Aha!" moment; God had revealed my problem to him. *Hallelujah! This has to be the key, finally!* I was tired and had no money.

The pastor continued, "You did not *NAME* your seed; you were not specific!"

When I heard this, I felt absolute despair: *God help me! This Christian thing seems too difficult.*

Obedience god immediately replied, "If you have put your hand to the plough and look back, you are not fit for the kingdom."

I wanted to cry; I was exhausted. It felt as if nothing was

working and that I would never be good enough to qualify before God. I took a deep breath, trying to encourage myself to start all over again. However, as I was remembering all that I'd gone through over the past six months, anger rose in my heart and I shouted at the pastor, "This is bullsh**! This tithing and sowing crap is killing me! What is wrong with God? Could He not care for me, as a father should? Something is wrong with this doctrine. Something is f*** wrong!" And I stormed out.

Within seconds, the following voices echoed in my head:

Righteousness god: "You said the f-word. Your seed is dead now, just before the breakthrough. You need to repent. I cannot use you in this state. You need to get your act together!"

Obedience god: "You have been disobedient; you said the f-word and the s-word. You are in rebellion against my leaders and my principles. Is obedience not better than sacrifices? You are backsliding. You are disobedient and you will have to bear the consequences!"

Ruler god: "Satan got to you this time. You need to fight him. There is no time for weariness. If you continue this way, there shall be no place for you in the army of God!"

Precept god: "Now you've done it! You've opened the door for the devil, so on principle I cannot help you. You opened the door!"

Kingdom god: "The kingdom suffers under this kind of behaviour. You need deliverance from demonic oppression. You are bearing the fruit of the flesh. You are in the flesh and need to get back into the spirit!"

Tears flooded my eyes as I got in my old car and drove off. Then, as I was driving away in despair, I heard the voice of my Abba—the one I loved and who had always loved me, "**Bertie, I love you, and you don't owe Me a cent. Please stop all this kind of giving and see how I prosper you. You are worth far more to Me than what you can ever do for Me.**"

I wanted to rebuke Satan, but feeling the pleasure of God flooding me through those words, I realized it could only be the voice of my Abba. Still, the other god-voices rose up in objection: "You cannot believe any word that contradicts Scripture! It is Satan speaking to you. Submit the word to the pastor and you will see him confirming it as Satanic …"

I interrupted, "Get away from me, Satan. I am finished with this tithing-and-sowing rubbish forever. I hate you. I am going back to the **place of peace!**"

Your Relationship with God Rests in His Person

In looking back at that time, I remember the pain of losing touch with my Abba, through my seeking after the "more" that came with the promise of riches. You cannot define relationship with God by the wealth He might want to give you. Your relationship with God rests entirely in His Person—the loving, caring, no fault-finding Father of our Lord Jesus!

When I read 1 Tim 6:10 again, I realized that I had missed verse 9:

But they that will be rich fall into temptation and a snare, and into many foolish and hurtful lusts, which drown men in destruction and perdition (*KJV*, 1 Tim.6:9).

In my longing to be rich, I experienced temptation, snares and many hurtful desires. The **destruction** this brought on me broke my back, as I have explained in this chapter. I had a good look at 1 Tim 6:9-10 again, and came to a completely different conclusion about what these verses actually mean. Let me now share this revelation with you.

CHAPTER 3

The Recovery Process

Peace flooded my heart as I drove away from the church office, rebuking Satan, leaving behind all his voices of accusation. As I drove, I realized I would have to study the Scripture that says the love of money is the root of all evil. But when I read it again, I still did not understand it any differently. It was just the same old verse stating that God does not have a problem with money, as such, but that the root of all evil is the LOVE of money.

It wasn't until some years later that the full truth of that verse struck me, which I will share in this book. It's interesting how the subconscious mind makes you see what you believe. I'm amazed at how blind I was to what is actually written in that verse, even after I renounced the lie on tithing. It was almost as if I could not read properly; I saw things that were not even written in the verse. I can't count how many times I read it before I came to the true understanding of it!

Looking back, I've come to the conclusion that the harm done to me, in believing the lie about money, could not be repaired by simply rebuking voices of accusation, or even by turning my back on tithing and the sowing-and-reaping system. Since it was through faith in that system that my belief about God had fundamentally changed, I had to have my heart reprogrammed or I would never understand Scripture correctly and enjoy a normal life again. I suffered a great amount of pain, my wrong belief torturing me for many years. The only way life could be restored to me was if the truth (right belief) could be restored to me. Unless the right belief of truth becomes common sense for us, we will be victims of the wrong kind of wisdom forever. I can think of a few words to describe my life when I lived by the wrong logic: *darkness*, *blindness* and *hell*. However, I never perceived it as blindness or darkness until I saw the light.

When I realized the lie that had found a pathway through the tithing and sowing-reaping teachings, there were several ways I could've responded. Rebellion against giving, as such, would not bring freedom for me. Hating church would only make matters worse. Anger towards those who introduced me to those teachings would just pull me deeper into the pit. The only answer was to hear a truth that is **believable**, based on facts about Jesus Christ and what He has done for me. Only then could all bitterness be healed, and my **view of God** and **who I am** be restored. That can bring forth true forgiveness in time. This is not a quick fix after years of harm.

Having knowledge of the truth does not change the subconscious mind the moment you hear it; God had to love me back to wholeness. I had to become accustomed to truth again. Since the Divine Ones function from a platform of love, resulting in trust, faith and other beautiful attributes, I had to get into a place where I could experience their life. I had to see and experience the love of God to the point that trust was formed in me. I needed to be in that atmosphere of life possessed by the Trinity, until their life permeated my thoughts and belief to the manifestation of their life in me. Furthermore, this life had to be the result of the living breath of God in me, and not my effort. This relationship-based change is not a five-minute process at all; it is a correction that will happen over time, effortlessly.

The best way to illustrate the dynamics a wrong belief had on me is to liken it to a **marriage**. Imagine you are happily married for five years, until a respected friend informs you that your wife recently had an affair. To make it worse, he provides evidence that she was cheating on you the whole time you were married! Suddenly your life is in pieces! But, after some serious introspection, you conclude that the fault is actually with you.

You read as many marriage and marital counselling books as possible, and earnestly consider ways to make her love you again, so that you can have the marriage you've always desired. In your desperation to restore the marriage, you become painfully aware of all your shortcomings, which then leads you to carefully formulate a set of principles and tasks you think will help to make the marriage work:

- Put out the trash daily.
- Wash the car twice a week.
- Buy her flowers once a week.
- Take the kids to school every day. Help with the dishes and laundry.

- Do not become angry with her when she is wrong.
- Take her on vacation at least once a year.
- Get the kids dressed in the mornings.
- Bring her coffee in the mornings.
- Listen attentively and show interest when she talks.

All of a sudden, the wonderful relationship you experienced dies. Love itself dies. The image you had of your wife and the way you use to look at her dies. Meanwhile, you become a slave of rules that you're convinced you must obey to keep the marriage working. Your definition of happiness even becomes distorted, and all this happens while you are being counselled by others.

Through all this effort, your perception of a happy marriage changes to *my wife only loves me when I do things for her*. Yet, you still smile and laugh, go on holidays, help out in the house, and take the kids to school. Your wife seems happy, but inside you have died a kind of death you cannot put into words. It feels as if the marriage has deteriorated from a passionate, loving, trusting relationship to a cognitive, wilful, decision-based arrangement, rooted in fear of divorce. Imagine living like this for another five years, seven years, or even ten years!

Then, one morning you receive a call from another friend who invites you for breakfast at his place. At the breakfast table, he shares some information that proves your wife never actually had an affair. The new evidence reveals that the stories of her supposed affaire were entirely false and twisted. At once, you are confronted with the fact that you were deceived into believing a huge lie about your wife!

Imagine returning home while contemplating this new information. The more you think about it, the more you realize you were deceived into believing she was unfaithful. Heartbroken, you acknowledge that you believed a terrible lie about your beautiful wife. Both joy and sorrow flood your heart. Although you are relieved to know the truth, remorse for the years deprived of trust brings you to tears. You were living in such an emotional hell, but it's finally over.

When you apologize to her, she fully accepts it without holding a grudge, for all the while she was flooded with love for you. She had always prayed that you would see the truth one day; she never wanted to let go of the marriage because of a lie. Your newfound life together is like you've gotten married all over again!

We can liken this story to what most people experience when they discover their freedom from wrong teachings about God. The hurt does not leave you the moment you discover that you were deceived. The law system has shaped its wrong belief into your heart, to the point that it would be absolutely natural to experience everything the husband in this story experienced. Like him, your emotions and actions will naturally be born from the disappointment and hurt you suffer from being deceived. When you hear the words *give*, *church*, *building, prosperity*, *missions* and *generosity*, you may have feelings of fear and anger rise up in your heart.

This is a normal response, yet it can be deadly if you remain at that place, since the life God will share with you is one giving generosity, kindness and faithfulness. You will be just as hurt and dysfunctional in your newly discovered 'freedom' from law, if the hurt of abuse continues. The same influence that brought pain and destruction to your life, when you believed the lie, will persist in being the father of your life. Anger over abuse never sets you free from it; it just aggravates it. The root of all the husband's pain and turmoil was the lie, not only during the time he believed it, but also afterwards. It was his belief in the lie that distorted his perception of marriage, and only a kind of reprogramming could restore his belief to the truth.

How are we restored to the truth about God and our relationship with Him? Healing will come by having a NORMAL atmosphere in which the heart and mind can be renewed over time—a season where you can experience the realities of a true and beautiful 'marriage' relationship with God. It is of the utmost importance for people to realize that ongoing bitterness and hatred, because of the fear and uncertainty of never being good enough before God, will keep them in captivity to what was killing them.

As we look at the following questions about the husband in our story, consider how the restoration process can work for you, when you have believed a lie about God:

- Did the subconscious mind of the man change the second he understood that she was not guilty?
- How do you think he would feel about marital counselling courses after this?
- How would he relate to the friend who gave him the false information?

- Would he feel totally at ease if his wife neglected some things he expected from her? (For example, what if she neglected to call him when she was out of town?)
- Would he have a moment of fear if she were to leave on a two-week business trip?
- How would his daily life change in regard to putting out trash, washing the car, buying flowers, taking the kids to school, assisting with household tasks, going on vacations, helping the kids get dressed, bringing her coffee in the mornings and attentively listening?
- How would the abuse we suffered affect our view on money and the church, and what is the recovery process to have a life that is not hurt-based?

In most cases, the marriage would not be back to normal for at least a few years. For a start, he would experience aversion towards all marital courses because he would associate them with pain and lies. He might have begun to hate holidays or taking his kids to school, for his subconscious mind connects all the good he has done to lies and abuse. In fact, his whole life could be greatly influenced by the **abuse of the wrong belief** he suffered, so his mind will need to be renewed towards trust in a truly satisfying marriage, where lies and the connected abuse do not exist.

He would have to come to a point where his reality would not be tainted by the aftershock of abuse, enabling him to enjoy the fullness he experienced before. It might even be that he would continue to do all the good deeds he has done in the house, only because of fear of being a bad husband, and not out of love for his wife. And if the man's innermost being could not be freed from consequences of the abuse he went through in believing the lie, it could even lead to divorce—the very thing he always hoped to avoid!

When we look at what the husband went through in believing the lie, it cannot be seen as anything but being abused by the lie he believed. Every effort he made out of believing the lie was forcing him to live a life for which he was never designed. This is abnormal use or abuse of a person. In the very same way, all who have believed a lie about money have experienced the abuse of the system. Every effort to get God to manifest His blessing was actually abuse. It's abnormal to live like that, when we have a loving, relational God who has given us everything for free.

Let's apply these thoughts to money:

- Does the subconscious mind of man change the second he understands that he was misled about finances?
- How would you feel about teachings about money since you have realized that you have been deceived?
- How would we relate to the people that gave us the wrong teaching? Could our way of treating them be ungracious?
- When we are in a setting where the truth about money is taught, could it be that we will have anger rise up in our hearts on account of the hurt we have experienced.
- How would our view on money and the church change due to the abuse we went through and what is the process for recovery of a life that is not hurt-

based?

In summary:

- A wrong belief about God causes absolute devastation.
- Experiencing the full effects of healing might take some time, since God does everything through relationship.
- Until you can see God in the light of family-orientated relationship, it will be impossible to have your heart healed.
- To live in bitterness towards the old system that used and abused you, can never be the way to a new life of true freedom.

CHAPTER 4

Being a Rich Jew

Some years ago I watched a program about the art of being a blacksmith. I have never known what blacksmiths actually do. All I knew was that it gets very warm in the room where they work with red-hot irons! As I was watching the program, I gained a considerable amount of knowledge and insight into what blacksmiths actually do. They are very artistic people who really **understand** steel and heat. The knowledge they have about steel, and its characteristics at certain temperatures, is the foundation from where their artistic abilities are unleashed.

They can tell, to the centigrade, how hot the steel is by its colour. This enables them to know exactly where to beat on the steel, and at what time in the cooling process, in order to gain the maximum strength from it. They will not keep the steel in the furnace a second too long, or too short, before starting to work on it. What seems to the outsider as just beating on a piece of hot iron is actually the stretching or shrinking of metal. Only a person who knows the characteristics of steel, at high temperatures, can do this in such a way. Any artistic person can beat a piece of steel with a hammer, but only a person who really **understands** metal and heat can use his creativity to form a sword, knife or perfect door hinge out of a block of metal. The key to the trade is the **specialist's knowledge and insight** into the nature of steel.

The Importance of Understanding

In the same way that blacksmiths understand steel and heat, if we want to walk in true freedom from all financial abuse, we need to **understand** the Kingdom of God and how it functions. We need to have hearts available for the truth— and only the truth. According to Scripture, the principle of understanding is directly linked to the truth bearing its fruit in our lives:

When anyone hears the Word of the kingdom and does not understand it, then the wicked one comes and catches away that which was sown in his heart. This is the seed sown by the wayside (*MKJV*, Matt.13:19).

But he that received seed into the good ground is he that hears the word, and understands it; which also bears fruit, and brings forth, some an hundredfold, some sixty, some thirty (*NKJV*, Matt.13:23).

It is very clear that Jesus connected *fruit* with *understanding*. Those who do understand the message of the cross, and the Kingdom of God, shall bear its fruit. But, those who do not understand it shall not bear fruit. I will further explain God's Kingdom in another chapter, but for now I would like to focus on the importance of *understanding*. In this chapter, I am going to explain the meaning of *the love of money*. Unfortunately, it will be a bit complex, and even dogmatic, but it will lead to the beautiful fruit of understanding. Let's stop and pray:

I pray that God will strengthen your inner man to see the dimensions of this truth of the Gospel. Amen.

After reading this book attentively, you will also understand why the love of money is the root of *all* evil and not just *some* evil. It will lay the foundation for understanding the teaching on financial provision in the Bible, taught by Jesus and recorded in Matthew 6. I will explain why "the *love* of money" has nothing to do with money, as such; yet, it would be nearly impossible to define it outside of money, not only for Jews, but also for 90 percent of Christians today.

A Common Jewish View on Money

16 And behold, one came and said to Him, Good Master, what good thing shall I do that I may have eternal life? 17 And He said to him, why do you call Me good? There is none good but one, that is, God. But if you want to enter into life, keep the commandments. 18 He said to Him, Which? Jesus said, You shall not murder, you shall not commit adultery, you shall not steal, you shall not bear false witness, 19 honour your father and mother, and, you shall love your neighbour as yourself. 20 The young man said to Him, I have kept all these things from my youth up; what do I lack yet? 21 Jesus said to him, If you want to be perfect, go, sell what you have and give to the poor, and you shall have treasure in Heaven. And come, follow Me.

22But when the young man heard that saying, he went away sorrowful; for he had great possessions. 23Then Jesus said to His disciples, Truly I say to you that a rich man will with great difficulty enter into the kingdom of Heaven. 24And again I say to you, It is easier for a camel to go through the eye of a needle than for a rich man to enter into the Kingdom of God. 25When His disciples heard, they were exceedingly amazed, saying, Who then can be saved?26But Jesus looked on them and said to them, With men this is impossible, but with God all things are possible (*MKJV*, Matt.19:16-26).

The most outstanding verses in the Bible, for what we need to understand about the Jewish concept of money, are verses 24-25 above. These verses reveal that the Jews linked the kingdom of the Messiah and salvation to money and the rich. The disciples were "**exceedingly** amazed." Or, some translations say they were "astonished **above measure,"** when they heard that it is difficult for a rich man to enter into the Kingdom of God. They were so amazed that they had to ask, "Who then can be saved if a rich man cannot be saved?"

The Jewish worldview is that the entire universe, including man, is created in such a way that people climb the ladder of perfection systematically. As man nears perfection, through his own efforts, God will help him attain a level that transcends his own limitations. Being set free from any nation that oppressed a Jew to attain to this so-called prosperity is, by the Jewish system, defined as "salvation," or the way to inherit the Kingdom.

The Jewish system promotes the belief that the more you live up to the standard of living described in the Judaic laws, the more the law justifies and frees you from darkness, sin struggles and poverty in this world. Darkness is seen as uncivilized living, as well as poverty. Non-Jews who do not obey the law are considered sinners. In this mind-set, **gain equals godliness.** One can only imagine the unhealthy **love of money** such a belief system brings forth!

Imagine the confusion, in the minds of the Jews, when Jesus told the story of the rich man and Lazarus:

19 *"There was a certain rich man who was clothed in*
purple and fine linen and fared sumptuously every day.
20 *But there was a certain beggar named Lazarus, full of*
sores, who was laid at his gate, 21 *desiring to be fed with*
the crumbs which fell[a] from the rich man's table.
Moreover, the dogs came and licked his sores. 22 *So it was*
that the beggar died, and was carried by the angels to
Abraham's bosom. The rich man also died and was
buried. 23 *And being in torments in Hades, he lifted up his*
eyes and saw Abraham afar off, and Lazarus in his bosom.
24 *Then he cried and said, 'Father Abraham, have mercy*
on me, and send Lazarus that he may dip the tip of his
finger in water and cool my tongue; for I am tormented in
this flame.' 25 *But Abraham said, 'Son, remember that in*
your lifetime you received your good things, and likewise
Lazarus evil things; but now he is comforted and you are
tormented. 26 *And besides all this, between us and you*
there is a great gulf fixed, so that those who want to pass
from here to you cannot, nor can those from there pass to

us.' [27]*Then he said, 'I beg you therefore, father, that you would send him to my father's house,* [28]*for I have five brothers, that he may testify to them, lest they also come to this place of torment.'* [29]*Abraham said to him, 'They have Moses and the prophets; let them hear them.'* [30]*And he said, 'No, father Abraham; but if one goes to them from the dead, they will repent.'* [31]*But he said to him, 'If they do not hear Moses and the prophets, neither will they be persuaded though one rise from the dead'"* (*NKJV*, Luke 16:19-31).

In the Jews' eyes, Lazarus personified an abomination for touching the dogs that licked his wounds. Jews were not to touch a dog, for it would make them unclean. Lazarus had nothing and nobody, and because he was sick, poor and waiting to be fed with the crumbs from the rich man's table, to the Jews, he was just as much a dog as the dogs who licked his wounds.

Jesus boldly declared that Lazarus opened his eyes in the bosom of Abraham, while the rich man found himself in Hell. This was a complete contradiction to the belief of that time, since it would be impossible for a rich Jew to go to Hell. To the Jews, Hell was for the ungodly, a place of purification from all ungodliness for a period of twelve months. Furthermore, it would be impossible for a poor, sick beggar, licked by dogs, to go to Heaven. To the Jews, the beggar was a beggar because of God's condemnation for his disobedience to the law. In a belief system where financial gain is a sign of godliness, **money is loved** and **poverty is hated**.

Imagine the spiritual suffering, and absolute slavery, in

which the poor of that time lived. Their poverty was seen as the public declaration of God rejecting their best effort to achieve the righteousness described in the law. The law could've freed them from their poverty and damnation, but instead, the poor and sick would have the fearful expectation of Hell for twelve months in the afterlife.

Legalism and confidence in riches were part of the same concept. Jews respected and honoured wealth as an indication of godliness and the desired manifestation of working the principles described in the Torah. If we can see that this unhealthy, legalistic view of *gain as godliness* is the opposite of what true Christianity stands for, we can have a much better understanding of what Jesus said about money.

Jesus Came to Preach the Gospel to the Poor

When Jesus said to the rich young ruler, "Sell all you have, give it to the poor and come follow Me" (Mk. 10:21), He was not at all saying that giving to the poor could save him. He was actually encouraging him to reject the system in which salvation is based on riches. He told the rich young man not to find his identity in the law, looking instead only to Him, Christ, for salvation. In other words, Jesus wanted the man to see the poor as rich and those that trusted in riches as poor. That is the beautiful new understanding we see in the New Testament that Jesus introduced. Let's look at some fascinating Scriptures about this:

"The Spirit of the Lord is on Me; because of this He has anointed Me to **proclaim the Gospel to the poor**" (*MKJV*, Luke 4:18, Isa. 61).

Jesus came to give good news to those who were seen as outcasts and rejected by God. He came to declare God's acceptance and love for all human beings, based on what He was about to do for them, and to declare that their situations were no indication of their acceptance, since righteousness would now be a gift from Him. He declared to the poor that they were just as accepted as the rich, since both rich and poor would be forgiven on the grounds of His work alone.

Do Not Trust in Uncertain Riches

"Charge the rich in this world that they be not high-minded, nor trust in uncertain riches" (*MKJV*, 1Tim.6:17).

Paul is saying here that the rich should not go back to Judaism, where they trusted in their riches, thinking that they were righteous and approved by God because they had money.

Imagine the instability there will be in the lives of people who find their definition of acceptance in how life treats them in the here and now. Life will only be as stable as your business; so how can you ever have internal peace? An ever-increasing desire for more money will flood your heart, becoming the platform from where you will make all your decisions. A hunger for the next key to prosperity and wellness will overwhelm your life, leading you to the deepest dungeons of legalism in your quest for the secret to higher prosperity!

In Chapter 2, you read about the instability that was in my life when I started to put my trust in riches. This is

what was actually killing me. Unknowingly, I was drawn into the old Jewish belief system where riches, health and wealth are the signs of true blessedness. The Law of Moses was all tangled up with the name of Jesus in my mind. This mixture caused havoc in my life!

The Rich are Poor

9 *But let the humble brother rejoice in his exaltation;*
10 *and the rich one rejoice in his humiliation, because he*
shall pass away as the flower of the grass (*MKJV*, James
1:9,10).

17 *Because you say, I am rich and increased with goods*
and have need of nothing, and do not know that you are
wretched and miserable and poor and blind and naked,
18 *I counsel you to buy from Me gold purified by fire, so*
that you may be rich; and white clothing, so that you may
be clothed, and so that the shame of your nakedness does
not appear. And anoint your eyes with eye salve, so that
you may see (*MKJV*, Rev. 3: 17, 18).

When we read the book of James and the Revelation of John, we can see that both are addressing the Jewish system where money is loved. Let the poor (humble) brother rejoice in his exaltation, for he has been elevated to righteousness, justified, saved and accepted by Christ's free gift rather than by implementing the Law. Rejoice, for poverty—as well as prosperity—has lost its voice in declaring you blessed, in the presence of the thundering voice of acceptance by the Word of God. John identified those who believed that justification before God manifests in prosperity, as the *blind*, *wretched*, *miserable* and *poor* (v. 18).

CHAPTER 5

The Root of all Evil

When I first understood the Jewish concept of money, as I described in the previous chapter, I also saw what Paul was getting at when he described the love of money as the root of **ALL** evil in 1Timothy 6:

1 Let as many as are servants under the yoke count their
own masters worthy of all honour, that the name of God
and the doctrine be not blasphemed. 2 And they that have
believing masters, let them not despise them, because they
are brethren; but let them serve them the rather, because
they that partake of the benefit are believing and beloved.
These things teach and exhort. 3 If anyone teaches
otherwise, and does not consent to wholesome words
(those of our Lord Jesus Christ), and to the doctrine
according to godliness, 4 he is proud, knowing nothing. He
is sick concerning doubts and arguments, from which
comes envy, strife, evil speaking, evil suspicions,
5 meddling, of men whose minds have been corrupted and
deprived of the truth, supposing that gain is godliness.
Withdraw from such. 6 But godliness with contentment is

great gain. [7]For we brought nothing into the world, and it is clear that we can carry nothing out. [8]But having food and clothing, we will be content. [9]But they who will be rich fall into temptation and a snare, and into many foolish and hurtful lusts which plunge men into destruction and perdition. [10]For the love of money is a root of all evil, of which some having lusted after, they were seduced from the faith and pierced themselves through with many sorrows. [11]But you, O man of God, flee these things and follow after righteousness, godliness, faith, love, patience, and meekness (*MKJV*, 1Tim. 6:1-11).

Paul was addressing financial issues in the church because the people were falling into arguments, abuse and fights about money. He confronted Christian slave owners and slaves who were fighting with each other, to the point of discrediting the faith, and linked their fleshly fighting to a love of money as the root. Paul was connecting pain and strife to teachings in the church, taught by preachers who had a love of money. He was pointing out the wrong doctrine of *gain as godliness*, as I discussed previously.

Let's look at this practically, for the here and now. I knew people in churches, where I was either the pastor or assistant pastor, who were business owners with over two hundred people working for them, some of which attended the same church. I found that the *gain is godliness* message was just as alive in their hearts—whether owner or employee—as it was in the early church.

One particular business owner complained about the high wages he had to pay his workers and about the government raising the minimum wage. Meanwhile, this very shrewd businessman, with millions in the bank, was buying expensive cars, going on regular overseas holidays, and frequently buying new properties. The more money he made, the more he testified of how God was blessing him. I wondered if he subconsciously considered his workers to be a threat to his godliness, since the more he had to pay them, the less he would have for himself.

His workers complained to me that he wouldn't pay them enough and said they wanted to be the *blessed of God* as well. Just as they saw no opportunity to become rich by working for this boss, he thought he could never be rich enough because of the high wages he had to pay them.

See how the teaching of *gain is godliness* can be the breeding ground for strife in a church? This is what the Apostle Paul was addressing with Timothy. He wisely connected the strife and evil thinking in the church to a specific doctrine being taught. Obviously, the love of money was the root of all kinds of evil happening between masters and servants, in the church to whom Paul addressed his letter.

Fortunately, Paul had the solution to their problems. He knew the Jews he was speaking to believed that all people were alive in Heaven before creation, then incarnated into human bodies on Earth. This would mean that people moved from a higher life to a lower life, and then back to the higher life when they died. Paul's explanation draws on a common understanding of that time, by pointing out that in the higher life, where people came from, gain did not define people, for we came into this world with nothing and we will go out taking nothing with us:

6But godliness with contentment is great gain. 7For we brought nothing into the world, and it is clear that we can carry nothing out. 8But having food and clothing, we will be content (*MKJV*, 1Tim. 6:6-8).

The most powerful way to have true peace and godliness in your life, and in the church, is to simply be content on account of a revelation of who you are in Jesus. We need to be content with having adequate food and clothing, and not use it as a standard by which we measure our godliness. Rather than finding your identity in gain, as the Jewish system does, embrace the truth that in your poverty you can be godly. This way you regard the sacrificial work Jesus accomplished, in His death and resurrection, as the foundation on which you declare yourself as godly, giving Him all the glory. Paul asserts that the value of a man does not depend on material possessions, reminding us that a person comes into this world with nothing and leaves with nothing.

***All* evil, not just *some* evil**

What amazes me, in Paul's correction, is that he says the love of money is the root of **all** evil; not just the root of the particular evil he was addressing, but ALL evil! It always confused me that money could be the root of *all* evil, since I knew evil was alive before the creation of Earth, long before money came into the world. I believe evil found its way into the physical world through Satan, and then Adam and Eve were **infected**.

Another Bible passage that I couldn't understand is in Ezekiel 28, about Satan before his fall; it twisted my brain into knots! Scripture says the multitude of his *merchandise* caused his fall. I could never understand how that could be possible, since Satan could not conduct any business prior to creation. Let's first look at what the Apostle Paul actually means when he says, "the love of money is the root of all evil," and then we will talk about Ezekiel 28:

9*But they who will be rich fall into temptation and a snare, and into many foolish and hurtful lusts which plunge men into destruction and perdition.* 10*For the love of money is a root of all evil, of which some having lusted after, they were seduced from the faith and pierced themselves through with many sorrows* (*MKJV*, 1Tim. 6:9,10).

Let's define the "love of money," in the terms used by the apostle Paul. It is significant that those who want to be rich fall into "temptation and a snare." Scripture states it clearly:

"But **they who will be rich** fall into temptation and a snare." (*MKJV*, 1Tim. 6:9).

"FOR (because) the love of money is the root of all evil." (*MKJV*, 1Tim. 6:10).

Do you want to be rich?

In my experience with doing business, and having many friends who are businessmen, I have seen the desire for riches change a person's business to a living hell. A businessman would take on jobs that consumed his time to the point that he would lose his family because of negligence. No human being is designed to live with such stress! A person grounded in a belief that causes love for money would accumulate debt and then stress himself half to death, should the interest rate on his loan rise. As the Bible says, he pierces himself through with many sorrows.

As described in the first chapter of this book, life is for man to enjoy; however, all joy is cut short when he gets to the point where he wants to become rich. This happens because of a change of belief, or rather, to believe what is contrary to God's belief. What I have experienced myself, and seen with many businessmen, is that you can enjoy life and your work until the moment you embrace the Christian "prosperity" teaching. Then all kinds of pain and strife start. The following example is just one of many ways it can manifest in people's lives:

There are many unemployed people who never seem to find a job. While they are "looking" for jobs, they live on the generosity of the church and family members. Even with bills piling up, they maintain that they are trusting God for a "breakthrough," which seems to always elude them. However, where jobs are available they don't apply, or they turn down a job offer because "it doesn't pay enough." In other cases, they'll apply for jobs they most likely won't get, considering their inadequate qualifications and lack of experience. What could be at the root of such behaviour?

It might be that they are basing their identities on the ideology that *material possessions and manifestation of blessings define you.* In that case, a low paying job would humiliate them, defining them as unblessed and defeated.

So they would rather live in debt and dependent on others, with the more acceptable excuse of being in the "process of finding a job." As a result, they live a life of always being in need, and unfortunately, others might even consider them to be lazy. Oftentimes, confusion sets in because God did not provide a job when they trusted Him for it. All kinds of pain and legalism then start to manifest and it becomes difficult to feel loved and accepted. Eventually, it becomes almost impossible to see good in anything or to expect any good to happen.

Stinginess Can Be Born from the Belief that Gain is Godliness

To me, it is very clear in Scripture that the *gain is godliness* belief manifests in the form of desiring riches, which is a perfect setup for an abundance of hurt, more deception and destruction. Since having a lot of money defines life for such a person, his subconscious mind experiences a false sense of security; this is when **stinginess** can easily settle in. Sometimes stinginess is an indescribable emotion, manifesting in a person's willingness to spend a lot of money on himself, but not on his employees or for upgrading the equipment they are using.

As a fruit of wrong belief, stinginess associates the feelings of acceptance and being successful with the spending of money on oneself. In that frame of mind, spending money on others means the loss of one's own prosperity, which causes feelings of rejection and insecurity. People may not even understand why they use all kinds of rationalizations to justify NOT spending any money on material things. On the other hand, in their stinginess, they will spend a lot of money on things that they think will define the blessedness of God on their lives.

When people believe gain is a sign of God accepting their obedience, they will hate "not having enough money," since it means God is rejecting their efforts of obedience. Having less will spell rejection from God when gain is seen as acceptance. Feeling rejected is one of the most destructive emotions known to man and will be avoided above all else. If you want to correct the belief of such a person— especially if it seems to be working for him— be ready for your correction to be seen as absolute heresy. Even just being told that he has believed something that's not correct can seem like rejection to him. The reason for such a strong reaction is that his subconscious mind connects anything that contradicts his current belief with rejection.

The forms in which stinginess can manifest are unending; **giving can even be a fruit of stinginess**. When a person believes *gain is godliness*, an overwhelming fear of lack (not having what he needs), can flood every fiber of his being. Imagine what could happen if this fear was combined with a teaching that says we gain financially by giving, like the sowing-and-reaping teaching, for instance. Although generous giving may occur, it will not be as a fruit of the Spirit, but because people are tortured by the fear of lack! Giving can never set a person free from stinginess. Let me say that again—giving can never set you free from stinginess!

We need to understand that a life of regularly giving does not necessarily mean a person is generous. Only one kind of giving can set us free from stinginess, and that's God's giving. God gave His Son, Jesus Christ, so that the power of sin could be broken over us. Those who believe and make use of this truth will experience freedom as intended by God. A person experiencing this freedom is introduced to the peaceable emotion and power of generosity that exists in the heart of God. True generosity is a fruit of understanding and believing grace.

Giving is powerless to set us free from stinginess and the death grip of loving money. This also applies to hoarding, saving, or even being "responsible," and "wise," with your finances. You will only find **real freedom** by understanding and believing the Gospel of God's love for you. Although the voice of insecurity can be very loud, we must never forget the inner voice of the Father, calling all people to truth. Although it might seem very soft and distant, it is persistent and penetrates the depths of one's being, should you not kick against the prodding of His voice (See Acts 26:14).

It is clear, from Scripture, that the force which drives us to desire riches is a certain **belief**. As a person believes, so he is (See Prov. 23:7). If you want to be rich, there is a belief behind it. I would like to expound on this particular belief, which Paul identified as the *root of all evil*. It is important to define it and see where Paul got the concept. We will also look at Ezekiel, where I believe we'll find confirmation that the New Testament passages we are talking about in this chapter reveal the **root belief behind all evil**, which Paul phrased as "*the love of money*."

In Paul's letter to Timothy, he used the particular Greek word *philos* for *love* (See 1Tim. 6:10). Philos describes the *friend of the bridegroom.* This phrase, which was common in Hebrew language and culture, is mentioned in Thayer's Dictionary in one of its definitions of the word *friend.* The *love of money* belief causes respect for money, which can also be called *friendship with* or *love for* money. The friend of the bridegroom's role was to ask the hand of the bride, on behalf of the groom, and then to render certain services in closing the marriage deal. The perfect metaphor! By befriending money, you are looking to it to *close the deal* on your marriage with God. Unfortunately, anything that *closes the deal* for you, outside of what God says, will destroy you. This is the instant you **fall away from being an "I am" to an "I might be," or an "I will become**." The same concept can be seen in Ezekiel 31, which we will discuss a bit later in this chapter:

1 Now it came to pass in the eleventh year, in the third
month, on the first day of the month, that the word of the
Lord came to me, saying, 2 "Son of man, say to Pharaoh
king of Egypt and to his multitude: 'Whom are you like in
your greatness? 3 Indeed Assyria was a cedar in Lebanon,
with fine branches that shaded the forest, and of high
stature; and its top was among the thick boughs. 4 The
waters made it grow; underground waters gave it height,
with their rivers running around the place where it was
planted, and sent out rivulets to all the trees of the
field. 5 Therefore its height was exalted above all the trees
of the field; its boughs were multiplied, and its branches
became long because of the abundance of water, as it sent
them out. 6 All the birds of the heavens made their nests in
its boughs; under its branches all the beasts of the field

brought forth their young; and in its shadow all great nations made their home.[7]Thus it was beautiful in greatness and in the length of its branches, because its roots reached to abundant waters.[8]The cedars in the garden of God could not hide it; the fir trees were not like its boughs, and the chestnut[a] trees were not like its branches; no tree in the garden of God was like it in beauty.[9]I made it beautiful with a multitude of branches, so that all the trees of Eden envied it, that were in the garden of God.'[10]"Therefore thus says the Lord God: 'Because you have increased in height, and it set its top among the thick boughs, and its heart was lifted up in its height, [11]therefore I will deliver it into the hand of the mighty one of the nations, and he shall surely deal with it; I have driven it out for its wickedness'" (*NKJV*, Ezekiel 31:1-11).

First, a word about spiritual interpretation of Scripture:

The objective I have in my explanation of the following passages is to explain that Pharaoh, Lucifer, the King of Sodom and the King of Tyre are all, when spiritually interpreted, pointing to Satan. I would like to show this so that we can, from a combined look at the fall of these kings, conclude how Satan fell.

There is a literal and spiritual interpretation of Scripture. Let's have a look at a wonderful example of a passage that was spiritually interpreted by John:

And their dead bodies shall lie in the street of the great city, which spiritually is called Sodom and Egypt, where also our Lord was crucified (*KJV*, Rev. 11:8).

The city is most likely Babylon, which is also referred to as the "Great City" (See Rev. 18).

When we read the above verse closely, we see that John also calls physical Jerusalem, where Jesus was crucified, "the great city," which is also Babylon (See Rev.18), and "**Sodom** and **Egypt**" (See Rev.16:19). Notice how John spiritually interprets Egypt, Sodom, and the place **where Jesus was crucified** as the GREAT CITY. The "great city," in the book of Revelation, points to Babylon.

According to Rev 11:8, we can say that Jerusalem, the city where Jesus was crucified, is Egypt, and it is Sodom, and it is Babylon. When we look at these cities and ask ourselves who the king of these cities could be, we can only conclude that it is Satan. Who is the King of Babylon other than Satan? Who is the King of Egypt represented in the Bible other that Satan? Who would the King of Sodom represent? They all represent none other than Satan himself.

Once we know how Satan fell, we will understand his wisdom and see how he is still operating today

When we take an in-depth look at how these kings came into being and then fell, we are able to gain insight into how Satan fell. Once we know how Satan fell, we will understand his wisdom and see how he is still operating today. I don't want to scare you or become a demon hunter, yet we can find wonderful insight from these passages that can be life changing and bring great understanding to the church.

When we look at the fall of the King of Babylon, we see a strong correlation between the King of Babylon and the King of Tyre (which is another example of a king that represents Satan when spiritually interpreted). With all this said, let's look at Ezekiel 28, to begin our investigation into why Satan fell:

11 And the Word of Jehovah came to me, saying, 12 Son of
man, lift up a lament over the king of Tyre, and say to him,
So says the Lord Jehovah: You seal the measure, full of
wisdom and perfect in beauty. 13 You have been in Eden
the garden of God; every precious stone was your
covering, the ruby, topaz, and the diamond, the beryl, the
onyx, and the jasper, the sapphire, the turquoise, and the
emerald, and gold. The workmanship of your tambourines
and of your flutes was prepared in you in the day that you
were created. 14 You were the anointed cherub that covers,
and I had put you in the holy height of God where you
were; you have walked up and down in the midst of the
stones of fire. 15 You were perfect in your ways rom the
day that you were created, until iniquity was found in you.
16 The multitude of your merchandise they have filled your
midst with violence, and you have sinned. So I cast you
profaned from the height of God, and I destroy you, O
covering cherub, from among the stones of fire. 17 Your
heart was lifted up because of your beauty; you have
spoiled your wisdom because of your brightness. I will
cast you to the ground; I will put you before kings, that
they may behold you (*MKJV*, Ezek. 28:11-17).

Now back to my explanation on what the *root of all evil* really is:

I believe this lamentation was written in a way that can help us understand what happened at the fall of Satan. The Spirit of God cleverly leads Ezekiel to use the word “merchandise,” in his description of the fall of the earthly king.

Merchandise means trade. Satan was trading holiness for prosperity. He traded great self-esteem for wealth. In his trading, Satan turned his identity into what he owned! I see this as the basis for the love of money being the root of all evil and see it in John 2:13-21 (especially vs. 16: “Do not make My Father’s house a house of *merchandise*!”)

The love of money being the root of all evil is when we trade the amount of money we have for the emotion of peace—when we trade our wealth for knowing we are loved by God. This to me, is the root of all works-righteousness. This belief is the foundation from where all works is born. The more we do, the better we have to trade for a good stand before God. The more good we do the more we can exchange the good works we have done for the emotion of having faith that it will go well with me in the future.

The **King of Tyre** possessed certain attributes that lead me to believe it could also be applied to **Satan**:

- He was perfect in all his ways in the day he was created.
- He was an anointed cherub.
- He was in the holy heights of God.
- He was in Eden, the garden of God, in the beginning.
- When we have a look at Lucifer, in Isaiah14, we find that it could easily be describing the same being. In

> Ezekiel 28, the King of Tyre is a shadow of Satan and in Isaiah 14, the King of Babylon is used as a type and shadow of Satan. Both these kings speak of the same being when spiritually interpreted. The King of Egypt would be the Pharaoh = Lucifer, the King of Babylon = King of Sodom = Satan. All of these kings are a type and shadow of Satan, just as the lamb, the scape goat, and the dove are types of Jesus.

The only "cherub," that could be described in this way is Lucifer. Lucifer (Satan) was perfect in the day that he was made and perfect in all his ways, until iniquity was found in him. Clearly, this "king of Babylon" is a type and shadow of Satan and his kingdom.

What was the *iniquity*?

...iniquity was found in you. The multitude of your merchandise they have filled your midst with violence, and you have sinned... (*Ezek*. 28:15, 16).

The *midst* is a way of saying the centre of a person's belief, or the heart. Scripture effectively says here that the "multitude of [his] merchandise" flooded his heart. Iniquity is described here as a belief that filled the core of Satan's being and manifested as "violence." The best way we can understand this is to link it with Isaiah 14 and Ezekiel 31. A closer study of these Scriptures reveals that *iniquity* is to believe you are defined and will have life by your ability and possessions:

9I have made him beautiful by his many branches, so that all the trees of Eden in the garden of God envied him.
10So the Lord Jehovah says this: Because you have lifted

yourself up in height, and he set his top among the thick boughs, and his heart is lifted up in his height (*MKJV*, Ezek. 31:9,10);

God made Satan great and beautiful. It was because of God, and not his own doing, that Satan was who he was. However, the problem came in when he began to find his identity in his high position, defining himself by the great things God had actually accomplished in and for and through him. In simple language, we can say that he defined who he was in all that God gave him. His heart, or belief—for with the heart we believe—was lifted up in the very height God had actually given him.

Satan was a perfect being; he was very rich, existing in the same domain as God, and having everything he could ever desire. According to Ezekiel 31, he was the greatest tree in the garden of God. When his heart was lifted up in his stature, iniquity flooded his heart and it corrupted him; thus, he fell from his holy position and his heavenly abode.

Since money did not exist in the Garden of Eden, we can substitute money for anything that would be the **friend that seals the marriage deal** between you and God. The belief that something outside of God *seals the deal* on your union with Him is the *iniquity* mentioned here, expressed as *the love of money or merchandise.* This is true even when the blessing or possession comes from God. Remember that Satan fell by finding his identity in the very thing God gave him. This was not just at a cognitive level but at a belief level. What caused Satan's heart to be lifted up? Or, in other words, in what was the heart of Satan lifted up? Here is the answer: in the abundance of his merchandise and blessedness. Let me say that again: in the abundance of his merchandise, Satan became proud and went away from God. This logic or belief-system is called *iniquity* and it is the root of all evil.

I need to say this again: The proof of sonship is not in what you possess as a son, but in **who** your Father is. The moment our hearts are lifted up in our stature, our belief tells us that what we possess, or how we perform, declares who and what we are. It is then that we have entered the logic of Satan and will come to a fall. This is when the wisdom of Satan enters us, and we start to have the love of money—friendship that seals the deal. Once we say we are blessed because God has given us possessions, or we say that being rich means we are the "blessed of God," and our wealth has *sealed the deal,* we have fallen in love with money, or with our achievements, or possessions. It doesn't matter what you call it; it all boils down to the same thing. We are not finding our identity in the Spirit of God anymore, but in the *abundance* that *He* brings into our lives. We walk outside of our original design, sinking into darkness and eventual death. Clearly, we can see that this is the root of **all** evil, since it is where all evil began, taking us away from trusting in God for everything we need.

The word *evil* can be defined as, "being filled with labors and annoyances," according to Thayer's Dictionary, and it leads to violence. The best way I would describe evil, in line with the revelation I have about grace, is as follows:

Evil is what you think needs to happen to create for yourself what only God can do in your life. In other words, evil is what people believe needs to happen to seal what

God already declares as true over them (Bertie Brits).

One of the worst things that can happen to a person is when a message that promotes iniquity and evil is preached to him, "in the name of Jesus." It is a way that seems unto life, "but its end is the way of death" (See Prov. 16:25).

The following verse in the book of Luke sums up the fall of Satan:

And he said unto them, Take heed, and beware of covetousness (love of money): for a man's life consists not in the abundance of the things which he possesses (*KJV*, Luke 12:15).

"Covetousness" here has the same root word found in the "love of money," from 1Timothy 6:10. Satan based his life on the abundance of his possessions, rather than on God. Satan's heart was lifted up in his beauty, which resulted in his fall.

The Emotion of Lack Always Accompanies the Law

There was a rich man who met with Jesus, who was very sincere (See Mark 10:17-25). He was really giving his best, in obedience to the law, to inherit the Kingdom of God. I believe he did all he had to do and still felt lack. Because of this, he asked Jesus what he still lacked. The emotion of *lack* always accompanies the law, and Jesus knew it, so He instructed him to obey the law. As recorded here for all believers afterward to read, the rich man said that he had kept the law from his youth but still lacked something. Jesus instructed him on how to be perfect. Perfection can only be obtained in following Jesus and rejecting the system by which you find your identity in the abundance of your possessions (as explained in Chapter 4).

(It might help you to read chapter 4 again. When I recently watched a movie for the second time, I gained more understanding of the background context and the pain and joys of the characters, as intended by the director and writer of the story. The same is true in reading a book; when we read something more than once, we get so much more from it.)

Jesus stated that it's very difficult for a rich person to enter the kingdom. This was true especially for the Jews, for their belief was deeply rooted in the abundance of possessions as the evidence of their obedience to the law, which they saw as the way to enter into the coming kingdom. Unfortunately, most church leaders today do not understand what the "love of money" is actually referring to. In our ignorance, Church, by preaching financial prosperity, we are making that which kills us the end goal of the Gospel! This is nothing but the "the lust of the eyes and the pride of life" (KJV, 1John 2:16). I believe most preachers who teach this do so ignorantly, but there are also those who see the true Gospel as a cancer in the church and would like to eradicate it, the sooner the better.

As I've already explained, "the love of money" includes **anything** that *seals the deal*, in our eyes, on our unity with Christ. As such, it is much more than money; it includes anything we look to for defining who and what we are. If we know it is God who supplies all good things for us, then how can our hearts be lifted up and proud about what HE has given us! So, whether God produces in us success at work and ministry, favour with people, or financial prosperity, the only true reference we will ever have of who we are is God Himself, not what He can produce in or through us.

Take the description of Satan in Ezekiel 31:1-10, for example. Spiritually interpreted, Satan is likened to the greatest tree in the Garden of Eden, but the real reason he was so great was because GOD planted him by the underground waters of many rivers. As the water was making Satan great and very beautiful, his heart was lifted up in his beauty; or in other words, he placed his trust in his own beauty, instead of the Spirit—the real source of his greatness. He started to define who and what he was by *what* the Spirit produced in him, and that became his self-image. For a great example of Satan's belief system, let's look next at what Jesus was going through when He was in the desert:

3 *And when the tempter came to him, he said, If thou be the Son of God, command that these stones be made bread.*
4 *But he answered and said, It is written, Man shall not live by bread alone, but by every word that proceeds out of the mouth of God* (*MKJV*, Matt. 4:3,4).

When Jesus was baptized, before heading into the desert, a voice out of Heaven said, "This is My beloved Son, in whom I am well pleased" (See Matt. 3:17). This was the Father's word about Jesus Christ. Jesus is the Son of God because God said so, and that's that! When God speaks, it is the truth.

The concept of being a son, in the Jewish culture, is different from what we have in the Western culture. According to Judaism, being a son is to be equal with your father, possessing what he possesses in all aspects of your life. As his son, you own what he owns and even have equal authority. Because the Father declared Jesus to be the Son of God as He came out of the baptismal water, Jesus is the Son of God. His identity and everything about Him is based only on the word spoken by God. This word—and nothing else—is what made Him great.

Following Jesus' baptism and God's declaration, Jesus went into the desert to be tempted of the Devil. It was in the desert that Jesus suffered a very hard time. He had no food and no one had followed Him. In this lonely place, where He no longer had people with Him, no needs He could meet—none of the things that would normally confirm His place in life and who He really was—Satan came along and tempted Jesus, by telling Him that He should do a miracle to prove His identity. The thinking behind this temptation was that the miracle could then *seal the deal* to prove Jesus was the Son of God. Jesus did, in fact, have the God-given ability to perform miracles, but that was not the source of His existence! Just look at what Satan said: "If thou be the Son of God, command that these stones be made bread" (Matt. 4:3).

It was not because He could turn stones into bread that Jesus was the Son of God. He founded His Sonship on the fact that God was His Father—not on the **ability** the Father gave Him! The truth of His life was not in the "abundance" God gave Him, but in what the Father said: "This is My beloved son, in whom I am well pleased" (KJV, Matt. 3:17). The Father declared this long before Jesus started to perform miracles!

Jesus was perfect in the day He was born. He was sinless and possessed all the power and beauty of God. If Jesus would've had a change of heart, no longer believing in the Word of the Father but instead in the beauty or ability the Father gave Him, He would have fallen just as Satan fell. In that case, the evil thing would've been to turn the stone into bread or to jump from the roof of the temple unharmed— having His identity based on His performance.

Remember *evil* means the hard labour by which one believes he shall have life. The *root of all evil* is defining yourself, and finding your life, by something God gives you, whether it's good health, wealth, special talents, gifts of the Spirit, performing miracles or any other fruit of the Spirit. The following sentence is very important and is basically the conclusion of what I am trying to bring across in this chapter:

Since we all need money all the time, it is the most common thing by which we are tempted to measure ourselves.

What went wrong?

By looking at the dynamics explained in these last chapters, I can understand where everything went wrong for me, and see how my life was dumped into a pool of despair years ago. To look back at what happened to me, I will quote from Chapter 2:

What I was learning from charismatic prosperity preachers was that it would be disrespectful if I did not want to become extremely wealthy, since Jesus died that I could have wealth. In that context, salvation could not be complete apart from the abundance of money and material possessions (*Jesus is the Tithe,* Bertie Brits).

Where it all went wrong in my life was when I began to believe salvation from poverty was the proof of my spiritual salvation. Even if I was a rich man, the same would have happened the moment I befriended money as the thing that would *seal the deal* on my salvation. Without going into more depth on how this evil system sucks you deeper and deeper into its claws of death, what I will say is that it's hell, compared to a love relationship with God, where Jesus is the final word on your life! The weird thing is, I experienced it as life while I was in it, confusing the what-to-do-to-have- more advice with the voice of God. I had to be delivered to see how bad it really was. I now realize that the zeal burning in my heart, to get big and rich, was actually the love of money and not a strong zeal for God. There is nothing wrong with being zealous, as long as it is according to the truth. I was at a place where a belief contrary to the belief of God had entered my heart, convincing me that my whole blessedness lies in the gifts God gives me, and that it defines me. I started to believe that "gain is godliness." Thus, I wanted to become rich, and as a result, I was pierced with many sorrows, as 1 Timothy 6 states. If I had a Rolex, I would think *God has blessed me*; if I had a big stage, I would be seen as *the blessed*; if I had no debt, I would know *I am free*; if people received healing, I would know *I am anointed.*

It is important to keep in mind that "the love of money" is actually a love or friendship with **anything** you consider to be *proof* that you are a saved and blessed child of God, needing nothing more. This wrong belief entered my life through a desire for being rich, at first, followed by a love of large audiences, miracles, gifts of the Spirit and everything supernatural. It brought me to a place where my life was flooded with the kind of pain and death that is Satanic. It's very sad to say that this wrong belief entered the church in the very same way, being preached as THE truth and destroying many people's lives. This wrong belief can lead to divorce, abuse, and all kinds of pain we never want to have in our lives!

There is nothing wrong with having miracles, the supernatural, an influential church, a big business, a great job or a lot of money, as long as those things do not have a say in your heart about who you are—or who anyone else is, for that matter. The moment any of that tries to take credit for your blessedness and anointing from God, you have entered darkness. It is the gateway for the flesh to bear its fruit in your life. When you believe that which God does not believe, you "err from the faith and pierce yourself through with many sorrows" (See 1Tim. 6:10). Such sorrows come from reaching for, and working to maintain, a life that would have the same power as God's. The pain comes from reaching for something that is unreachable— it's unbearable! Yet, it is correctable, should we let go of the lie and go back to Jesus as the final word about us.

I did not realize I was yielding to an evil system with the *love of money* at its core, when I was seeking Jesus! I honestly desired to have all God wanted for me, but my sincerity could not protect me against the death contained in a system where financial gain and material possessions *seal the deal*.

CHAPTER 6

Provision God's Way

"But seek first the Kingdom of God and His righteousness; and all these things shall be added to you" (*MKJV*, Matt. 6:33).

In this chapter, I will explain the difference between the Jewish and Christian concepts of the Kingdom of God. If we first need to seek the kingdom, we must define the kingdom or we will not know what to seek. I remember the days when I would fast and have hours of prayer, "seeking the kingdom." I had no idea what I was doing, but thought *this must be how one seeks the kingdom*. What I was actually doing was advancing in the kingdom of darkness, rather than the Kingdom of God! What I did could best be explained in the words of Paul in Rom 10:

1 Brethren, my heart's desire and prayer to God for Israel is
that they might be saved. 2 For I bear them record that
they have a zeal of God, but not according to knowledge.
3 For they being ignorant of God's righteousness, and
going about to establish their own righteousness, have not
submitted themselves unto the righteousness of God (*KJV*,

Rom. 10:1-3).I was living the same passionate, zealous life as those who were seeking their own righteousness, anticipating how God would add to my life whatever I needed, after the *seek meter* in Heaven hit green for go. I thought He would add all things to me if I were to seek Him enough, but my searching only ended in the manifestation of bad fruit that comes from a wrong belief system. Let me clarify: for us to grasp what Jesus meant in Matthew 6:33, we need to understand that the Kingdom of God existed long before the earth was made.

The Basics

The Matthew 6 verses I'll explain in this chapter will be easy to understand, now that we've discussed what "the love of money" means. As we read it attentively, we will see how it is all about doctrine and belief. I will highlight key words that are important for understanding.

Before God made any creatures, He first provided what they needed to live on. Starting with the atmosphere, He created light and placed the sun in the universe, then the plants on Earth, then the plant-eating animals. He first created the seed-bearing herbs and fruit trees, then the human being. From the beginning, all provision has always been something that flows freely from God. He is not ignorant of our needs. He knows your every need and loves you dearly!

I was never concerned about whether I would have food or go hungry, until I got into the prosperity gospel. Suddenly, I was worried not only about having enough to eat, but also what *kind* of food I ate! And the same with my clothes; I became very concerned about WHAT I wore, when before I didn't even worry over IF I'd have clothes to wear. I no longer cared that I had a dependable car to drive; all that mattered was WHAT KIND of car I drove.

In the "prosperity by following principles gospel", it's about what car you drive, what clothes you wear, and what laptop you use. God knows these needs and He will provide it anyway. I remember the guilt I felt when I heard that Matthew 6:22-33 means not to worry WHETHER you will have clothes, shelter, and food rather than WHAT you wear or eat. The Lord said why are you worried? You shouldn't worry, so the verse was not the wonderful confirmation of God caring for me. Read Matthew 6 carefully. It states that we should not worry about WHAT we will eat or WHAT we will wear. Do I wear NIKE? Do I have Lucky jeans? Do I eat MacDonald's or steak in a fancy restaurant? The death is in the belief that the "WHAT" is what's important.

God's Purpose is for You to Share in His Kingdom and Partake of All its Provisions

I felt condemned by one of the most beautiful passages in the Bible because of a lack of understanding. We need to realize that Jesus is not trying to get us to believe **for** prosperity, but just **in** Him. He already knows your every need anyway. The practicalities of the Gospel are not to get God to provide for you. He has already committed Himself to provide for you. God's purpose in the Gospel is for you to share freely in His Kingdom and partake of all its provisions. Let's look at Matthew 6:

22 *The light of the body is the eye. Therefore, if your eye is*

sound, your whole body shall be full of light. 23*But if your*
eye is evil, your whole body shall be full of darkness. If
therefore the light that is in you is darkness, how great is
that darkness! 24*No one can serve two masters. For*
either he will hate the one and love the other, or else he
will hold to the one and despise the other. You cannot serve
God and mammon. 25*Therefore I say to you, Do not be*
anxious for your life, what you shall eat, or what you shall
drink; nor for your body, what you shall put on. Is not life
more than food, and the body more than clothing?
26*Behold the birds of the air; for they sow not, nor do they*
reap, nor gather into barns. Yet your heavenly Father
feeds them; are you not much better than they
*are?*27*Which of you by being anxious can add one cubit*
to his stature? 28*And why are you anxious about*
clothing? Consider the lilies of the field, how they grow.
They do not toil, nor do they spin, 29*but I say to you that*
even Solomon in his glory was not arrayed like one of these.
30*Therefore if God so clothes the grass of the field, which*
today is, and tomorrow is thrown into the oven, will He
not much rather clothe you, little-faiths? 31*Therefore do*
not be anxious, saying, What shall we eat? or, What shall
we drink? or, With what shall we be clothed? 32*For the*
nations seek after all these things. For your heavenly
Father knows that you have need of all these things. 33*But*
seek first the Kingdom of God and His righteousness; and
all these things shall be added to you (MKJV, Matt. 6:22-
33).

Understanding the Kingdom

Let me give a bit of historic background on what the Jews believed about the end of the world and their purpose on Earth, from Romans 2:

*17Behold, you are called a Jew, and rest in the Law, and
boast in God; 18and know His will and approve the things
excelling, being instructed out of the Law; 19and
persuading yourselves to be a guide of the blind, a light
to those in darkness; 20an instructor of the foolish, a
teacher of babes, who have the form of knowledge and of
the truth in the Law* (*MKJV*, Rom. 2:17-20).

Since the Talmud is the central text of mainstream Judaism, let's look at what "the Kingdom of God" means in the Talmud? It is believed to be **the refining of the body and the physical world, through the uplifting of the soul in obedience to the law**. The Jews see the world as darkness and the soul of man as the lamp. The belief is that they are to enlighten the world through the law, which to them is the way unto life. In fact, they believe the law is the only truth, and once obeyed, life itself. The only way refining of the body and the physical world is understood by the Jews is in having riches and all kinds of prosperity, as mentioned in passages like Deuteronomy 28:

*1And it will be, if you shall listen carefully to the voice of
Jehovah your God, to observe and to do all His
commandments which I command you today, Jehovah
your God will set you on high above all nations of the
earth. 2And all these blessings shall come on you and
overtake you, if you will listen to the voice of Jehovah your
God. 3You shall be blessed in the city, and be blessed in the*

field. [4]*The fruit of your body shall be blessed and the fruit of your ground, and the fruit of your cattle, the increase of your cows, and the flocks of your sheep.* [5]*Your basket and your store shall be blessed.* [6]*You shall be blessed when you come in, and blessed when you go out* (*MKJV*, Deut. 28:1-6).

According to Deuteronomy 28, life is found in prosperity, health, and wealth—a life consisting of the abundance of your possessions. So, man must be obeying the law in order to be blessed in the city and in the field, have healthy children and big crops, have a full storehouse, and so forth. The Jews believed that the finer the life they lived, the more they refined the world. This helped them to feel they were living up to the intent of the Talmud.

As a fervent student of the law and the traditions of the elders, Paul comes to an extraordinary conclusion, documented in Romans 7. He concludes that although the law seems to be the way to earn a good life, the end of it is death. Paul also boldly declares in Romans 7 that the law possesses no power to bring life to his human body, and therefore it is powerless to bring **refining to the physical world.** Eventually, he calls the law system—for the purpose of refining all things—weak and unable to bring purification! (See Rom 8:1-4). He even goes so far as to call those that try to live by it "lost and blinded by the God of this world" (See 2 Cor. 4:4).

To the Jews, there was nothing spiritual about the Kingdom of God; to them it was a physical kingdom of this world. They understood it as the Kingdom of the Messiah, who was a man that would come and deliver them from the oppression of other nations. They never viewed this Kingdom of the Messiah as a kingdom where righteousness is a gift, nor did they even consider complete perfect forgiveness as a free gift. **Salvation,** to the Jews, is what happened in Egypt when God saved them from the hand of the Pharaoh. They believe that when the Messiah comes He will bring world peace, all people will follow the precepts of the law, and through obedience to the law—as the Messiah enforces it on all nations—peaceful civilization will spread.

To the Jew, salvation means to be free from the oppression of all nations so they can freely obey the law. (This is not true for all Jews today, for many have become atheists.) According to this tradition, the kingdom is observed through **what** you wear and **what** you eat. Unfortunately, what the Jews believe is accepted in many churches, where people think that the wealth of the wicked is laid up for the just. This concept has even flowed over into the modern Pentecostal, Charismatic church. It is believed, in many churches, that the New Testament church will take over the world and refine it, by high moral values and the anointing. Yet, this is not going to be the case, since the Kingdom of God does not come in the form of the church perfecting the world. Perfection is what we hope for, with a confident expectation in the return of Jesus.

Let me summarize this concept:

The Jewish belief is that "salvation" means to be saved from anything that might stop you from receiving the blessings of obedience to the law, since true life is via obedience to the law. It is also believed that sanctification of the mind, and life by obedience to the law, will bring the development of civilization and political world peace. Thus, the Jews believe that they are the guide to the blind, that salvation— or let's call it development and world peace—is of the Jews through obedience to the law, resulting in great financial blessings and all kinds of prosperity. These blessings would then enable people to bring peace through civilization and obedience to the law.

I hope you can see how this view can only lead to a very unhealthy and unnatural outlook on money, which is the Kingdom of God amounting to no more than a measure of wealth and rulership over others. This would be a pitiful kingdom, where the law of God is enforced on all nations as the way, the truth and the life, with only the rich people holding the prominent positions.

The New Kingdom

With this in mind, we can only imagine the havoc the Gospel of John must've caused, when John called the Jewish people and their ways, "people walking in darkness, rejecting the only light" (See John 3:19). Conversely, John called Jesus, "the light of the world that enlightens every man," be he a Jew or a Gentile (See John 1:9). John was only elaborating on what Jesus was actually saying. Jesus said that the light of the body, that which will illuminate the body and the physical world, is the revelation you have, or the way you perceive things:

20 *And when he was demanded of the Pharisees, when the*
Kingdom of God should come, he answered them and said,
The Kingdom of God come not with observation:
21 *Neither shall they say, Lo here! Or, lo there! For,*

behold, the Kingdom of God is within you (*KJV*, Lk.17:20, 21).

The best way I can explain the Kingdom of God is to call it "the place of Trinity reality," as we discussed in chapters 2 and 3. It's a "place," where everything happens in relationship between the "Divine Ones," in the Godhead. The place where "let's" can take place by mutual influence and equal persuasion, unto the manifestation of the life that is possessed by Elohim in all who enter and partake of it. The Kingdom of God could be described as the framework on which dynamics that exist in the Trinity are built. I would not be surprised if some of you ask if such a place could ever exist for humans. Could we ever enter that place? Is that possible in the here and now? Yes. The answer is yes, and yes for all!

What I am about to share with you has changed my life and given me a sense of cleanliness and holiness that can only come from Him. I explain this, in detail, in my book, *Born from Innocence*, if you would like a more in-depth study of it. Here is a shortened version:

The Baptism of Jesus

I have always wondered why Jesus was baptized. I can remember thinking that God told me to be baptized because Jesus was my example, so I had to do what He had done. Later, I realized that it could never have been God saying those things. As I came to understand the baptism of John and the kingdom that was now at hand, I saw that those Scriptures actually have nothing to do with me getting baptized into water. There is something much greater, much bigger, hidden in John and what he declared.

It was so big that John announced the Kingdom of God is at hand, which meant that the Kingdom of God is here!

The Baptism of Jesus Marked the Beginning of the End of the Law Era

I never understood that there were many people baptizing in the days of John the Baptist; many people were making disciples of the Gentiles. In about 150BC, the Jews were making disciples out of the Gentiles, who would be baptized, circumcised and given the law as the enlightenment unto life. Since all Gentiles were seen as sinners and unclean, only they could be baptized, confessing their sin in the baptism, signifying that their sins would be washed away as they became part of the Jewish system of sacrifices. This conversion was also what was known to be a new birth where people were born into the ways of the law.

What made the baptism of John so extraordinary was that, unlike the Jews who baptized only Gentiles, he baptized Jews, which was completely taboo in those days. A Jew was never considered to be a sinner like a Gentile. Yet, John's baptism was for sinners only, so even the thought of being baptized, with the baptism of sinners, was an absolute disgrace to the Jew. When the Pharisees came to John and asked him who he was and why he would do such a thing, John boldly proclaimed that being a Jew means nothing to God for *"God is able to raise up children to Abraham from these stones" (MKJV, Matt. 3:9).*

The Jews didn't realize that they also needed the fruit of righteousness and freedom from sins, which accompanies repentance from believing in the old kingdom dynamics. Just as Paul taught in his letter to the Romans, John preached that all people—Jews and Gentiles alike—are sinners and guilty before the law. This was unthinkable for the Jews of that time! Nonetheless, John persisted in declaring that all people in the world needed forgiveness for the remission of sins, Jews and Gentiles alike. Since John preached no other kind of baptism but of repentance for the remission of sins, any person baptized by him was consenting to the fact that he was **a sinner and in need of repentance**. Imagine the baptism scene in one of those old movies: Jesus hikes out to the Jordan River where a wild man, John the Baptist, is baptizing people. A large crowd has gathered around John, who is taking no nonsense from the Pharisees, shouting and rebuking them for being hypocritical. All of a sudden, everything becomes very quiet as the cameras focus in on Jesus who is now walking right into the water. The people stare silently at Jesus as John baptizes Him; then, out of Heaven flies a dove, and it lands right on Jesus' shoulder. The baptism of Jesus is so beautiful and loaded with power! There is something so powerful about this event that we can feel yet not explain.

Let me explain this further. Years ago, we were doing an outreach in eastern Malawi, where there are predominately Muslim people, living in villages, and many of them are uneducated. Most of them have never heard of the baptism of Jesus and what it means. As a matter of fact, they were taught to be against the Christian faith, and were hearing the message of Jesus for the first time, when we preached to them. I remember, as we pitched our Jesus film projector and started to show the movie, the people were dead quiet. They all just watched intently from the beginning of the film until the baptism of

Jesus, when as He came up from the water they smiled and clapped their hands spontaneously.

This was so strange; why would these Muslim villagers respond this way? It was not normal. I could only conclude that they felt what all of us feel when it comes to the baptism of Jesus. We just have a wonderful feeling about it. It's a pleasing impression that brings a kind of peace, although the cognitive mind is unable to explain it. We don't understand why we are happy when we see this, yet there is some kind of an inner resonance telling us that it should be that way. Although this powerful impact of Jesus' baptism is mysterious, it does not leave us without understanding. I believe the power and mystique of the baptism of Jesus *is* revealed and it is all about the Kingdom of God. The way God does things was about to come to Earth. The reality of the Trinity was about to manifest on Earth, giving all people the opportunity to taste what true life is all about. Let's see His baptism more closely.

Closer to the Kingdom

One day, John sees Jesus walking on the banks of the river and reveals something very amazing, by the Spirit of God, "Look! The lamb of God that takes away the sin of the world" (NKJV, John 1:29).

What an outstanding statement! After he had just shouted out to the crowds that all people need to repent, John points to Jesus, claiming that He is the lamb that will take away the sin of all people. He has just contended that all people are sinners, and now in the same breath, he's announcing that all sinners' sin will be taken away in one Man, by one sacrifice.

Then, the unthinkable happens—something John could never have imagined in a million years! Jesus, the sinless Lamb of God, walks into the water to be baptized by John. John was declaring all people sinners, in need of repentance, and now Jesus, the sinless one, wants to be baptized into what John is announcing? How could this be! And what does this mean for us? Let's go on.

John then proceeds to correct Jesus and refuses to baptize Him:

14But John restrained Him, saying, I have need to be baptized by You, and do You come to me? 15And answering Jesus said to him, Allow it now, for it is becoming to us to fulfill all righteousness. Then he allowed Him (*MKJV*, Matt. 3:14, 15).

To *restrain* means to *utterly prohibit*. John, as radical as he was, utterly prohibited Jesus from being baptized, for he knew what it implied. John told Jesus that he needed to be baptized by Jesus, and not Jesus by him, for it felt completely wrong to baptize the innocent Lamb of God into the category of "sinner repenting of his sins." Jesus was holy, innocent, and perfect; how could it ever be that Jesus could be baptized with the baptism of the sinner? John thought this needed to be stopped! Jesus replied, "*Allow it now, for it is becoming to* **us** *to fulfill all righteousness*" (MKJV, Matt. 3:15). As John heard these words he allowed Jesus to be baptized.

It is amazing to see that Jesus uses the word "us," when he says, "for **us** to fulfill all righteousness." Jesus could not fulfill **all righteousness** unless John was involved. He had to be baptized by John for the kingdom of Heaven to be at hand. The kingdom that all people were living in was the kingdom of being sinners and under the power of sin, always falling short of the glory of God. It was a kingdom in which you had to use your willpower and obey laws to attain to life. The Kingdom of God, and the rule that is in the Godhead, is one where none of the Divine Ones has sin. Therefore, in order for that to be true on Earth, the sin of all people will have to be taken away.

When Jesus, the perfect innocent Lamb of God, was baptized with the baptism of the sinner, He took the sin of all people upon Himself. All sin was now received by Jesus, for He baptized Himself into the word that John was proclaiming. John declared all people sinners. Since Jesus did not have any sin, but was then baptized by John into sin, whose sin would then be on Him but the sin of all people?

It was not until after the baptism of Jesus, that He taught the Kingdom of God has now come to man. The rule that is in Elohim, by which His righteousness can now be ours, has come to Earth, for Jesus has taken the sin of the world upon Himself. From that day on, Jesus healed people, for healing is equal to forgiveness, declaring that sin is now on Him and not on the people anymore:

5 *For which is easier? To say, Your sins are forgiven you, or to say, Arise and walk!* 6 *But so that you may know that the Son of Man has authority on earth to forgive sins, then He said to the paralytic, Arise, take up your bed and go to your house* (*MKJV*, Matt. 9:5, 6).

The Kingdom of God

The Kingdom of God is the place where the rule of God exists in perfect love and innocence, where the will of God is done as in Heaven. On Earth, people try to do the will of God by obedience to laws. But in Heaven, it is done in the power of love, resulting in faith, belief in one another, and other godly characteristics. It is a unique realm where the righteousness of God is the only righteousness and it's available to all. It is the place where divine ones share in the life of *The* Divine Ones.

Jesus came and preached the Kingdom of God. Being made sin for us all, He pronounced thousands forgiven by every miracle He performed. The miracles testified to the fact that the new rule was already present—that sins are not on people anymore but on Jesus, who was carrying the sin of the world. This was made possible when Jesus was willingly baptized into the sin of the world.

For a detailed explanation of all of this, including the significance of the shedding of blood, please see my book, *Born from Innocence*.

Back to Seeking the Kingdom of God

"But ***seek*** *first the Kingdom of God and His righteousness; and all these things shall be added to you"* (*MKJV* Matt. 6:33).

With the new kingdom defined, we can elaborate on this verse:

Seek, according to Thayer's definition, means to *seek [in order to find out] by thinking, meditating, reasoning, to enquire into* … the Kingdom of God and His righteousness and all these things shall be added unto you (Matt 6:33).

Let's *meditate*, *reason* and *inquire* into how righteous Jesus is and how the new kingdom includes us. Let's **seek** how we are forgiven. Let's **seek** how innocent we are and how we are united in the sacrifice of the Lamb. And, as we seek by meditating, reasoning and inquiring, we will find that the things we were seeking under the law system will just be added to us effortlessly—Matthew 6:33, paraphrased.

We will miss the point of Matthew 6:33 if we try to use it as the magic key to get rich. Its purpose is much greater, in that it tells us that God's provision for all people is a given. We don't need to use this—or any Bible passage—to gain wealth, when we know God provides for us as our Father, in a relationship in which money is not what defines us. In our relationship with Him, His provision naturally floods our lives and our Abba, becomes alive to us as a loving Father and not a lawmaker again.

The first thing that happens, as we enter the kingdom, is an experience of the sweet fruit of **contentment**. I have found we think much more sensibly about business and money the moment the satanic system of, *I am what I possess* is removed from our belief. We find that there is an inner wisdom and contentment that saturate our lives, to the point that we cannot be forced into business deals we never wanted to make. It is very difficult to tempt a contented person into something he or she does not really want to do. God-based provision is also not seen as sitting lazily at home waiting for God to provide for you. Unfortunately, there are some people that think grace is all about not working a job since God is caring for them now.

I believe many jobless people will find jobs, or creative ideas through which they can be provided for, once they believe they are not defined by what they do or how much they earn. A person is freed from all stress and bondage in the mind the moment contentment settles in, as a result of believing the truth. It is enjoying life no matter what you do, not finding your identity in your work, and trusting in God who provide for you. It's a state in which all your attention is not directed to what you do for a living—while you are doing it.

Paul was so radical, in his message about the Gospel, that he even told slaves not to be bothered by the fact that they are slaves. How crazy is that! It's actually not crazy at all; it's pointing to something that is greater than this life. It's pointing to a contentment that supersedes all things we have ever seen or heard. It is directing us to a place where the deepest joy can be experienced. Paul did advise, though, that a slave should take the freedom when it comes his way. I am not promoting slavery here, but simply explaining the dimensions of the power contained in godly provision. Contentment is the foundation from where we can all live, while God meets our needs. Contentment is not the acceptance of poverty but enjoying life where you are, as God cares for you.

I close this chapter with a verse that needs no explanation in regard to godly provision:

"But my God shall supply all your need according to His riches in glory by Christ Jesus" (*MKJV*, Phil. 4:19).

CHAPTER 7

Entering the Kingdom of God

The most beautiful, most wonderful, life-giving kingdom has come to Earth! It is the kingdom of the Divine Ones, available for all people; yet, we find that there are many not seeing nor experiencing the kingdom in their everyday lives.

When I was living in my endless search for life, as explained in Chapter 2, I thought I understood and was partaking of the Kingdom of God. As a matter of fact, I was even trying to advance the kingdom and see the church take over the world. I would get up early in the mornings, binding the Devil and demons, and declaring the Kingdom of God over various towns, in hopes that Christians would rise to high positions in government and other key offices. I wanted all people to come to our church so that they could enter the kingdom. I did everything a good Christian in the Charismatic, Pentecostal church world would do to promote the Kingdom of God. I thought entering God's kingdom meant that people must confess their sins so God could forgive them, receive the Holy Spirit, and start winning souls through signs, wonders, and miracles. I saw myself as a kingdom worker and wanted all people to be as I was. The truth is, I was radically doing all these things with no clue of what the Kingdom of God is really about. I couldn't see the kingdom nor could I enjoy my life in it. My only understanding of God's kingdom, that came anywhere close to what it actually is, was that I believed I would be with Him when I died because of the blood of Jesus and His love for me. Unfortunately, while I could see only this small glimpse of the kingdom, I was actually living in the kingdom of darkness, even though I was claiming everything, "in the name of Jesus!"

I was blinded by the *love of money*, and driven by my zealous obedience to the methods for successful Christianity, proposed by the latest "revelation" of key preachers. Truth be told, what I wanted most of all was to reach that place where God actually wanted me. But, I was blinded by the law that was clothed in a Pentecostal, Charismatic cloak. I could not see the kingdom nor could I enter it. I was as I described in the beginning of this book: "The noise of legalism drowned out the voice of my Abba."

The Kingdom of God is not characterized by how big your ministry is or how many get saved at your meetings. It is not about getting your prayers answered, or having a healthy body, or giving to the poor. As a matter of fact, the Kingdom of God is not even determined by all people living holy. Even if everyone repented of sin and lived a good life, it still wouldn't mean that they see the kingdom and live in that which God really intended for us. Even if you could live perfectly sinless, that is no indication that you have entered the Kingdom of God. So, how can we, as humans, experience the realm where the Divine Ones dwell? How do we enter Elohim's reality and the dynamics that encompass the Godhead? One of the best known verses in the Bible is found in the third chapter of John. It is so powerful and really worth studying in depth. By looking at verses 1 through 16, we will realize how we can see and enter the Kingdom of God. I will explain my understanding without elaborating too much. For a more detailed explanation, you can read my first book, *Born from Innocence*. Before I get into John 3:16, I need to explain the concept of **birth** found in John 1:

12 But as many as received him, to them gave he power to become the sons of God, even to them that believe on his name; 13 Which were born, not of blood, nor of the will of the flesh, nor of the will of man, but of God (*KJV,* John 1:12, 13).

According to this passage, we have the right to be called "sons of God," when we have received Jesus, and we are those who are **born of God**. The best way I can translate these two verses is as follows:

John 1:12 All people, Jew or Gentile, that have grabbed a hold of Jesus, those that grabbed a hold of what His name really means as Saviour, with the purpose to make use of Him and what He concludes, and those who see what He accomplished as fully applicable to them, have the authority to say the wonderful life they have and live originates from God and is His life. These are those whose minds are at rest, having full satisfaction in what He accomplished on behalf of mankind

John 1:13 They don't owe the birth of this wonderful new life they have and its manifestation, in and through them, to the fact that they are of a certain ethnic group, nor to will power in obedience to commandments prescribed by Moses, nor to their craving for eternal life. They owe their birth, the life they possess in spirit and manifestation, to God birthing all He is and all He feels and enjoys into them, making what they have fully received God authentic and not a man-made counterfeit of original life (Bertie Brits).

When we are born from something, it has access to our lives and actually lives in and through us. If we look at a person—let's say a woman who's been really hurt in an abusive relationship and living in the hurt for many years to follow—we can conclude that she owes her life to the hurt and abuse she suffered. The life she lives is a direct result of what she believes about the abuse. What she believes about the abuse is what actually gives the abuse power to live in her, and we can safely conclude that her thoughts and actions have **hurt** as their father.

With this in mind, we can look at what John 3 talks about in connection to the *born again* experience. It's really important to understand this concept, for we will not be able to see nor enter the Kingdom of God unless we are born again. Let's read John 3:1-16:

1 There was a man of the Pharisees, named Nicodemus, a
ruler of the Jews: 2 The same came to Jesus by night, and
said unto him, Rabbi, we know that thou art a teacher
come from God: for no man can do these miracles that
thou doest, except God be with him. 3 Jesus answered and

said unto him, Verily, verily, I say unto thee, except a man be born again, he cannot see the Kingdom of God. 4Nicodemus saith unto him, how can a man be born when he is old? can he enter the second time into his mother's womb, and be born? 5Jesus answered, Verily, verily, I say unto thee, except a man be born of water and of the Spirit, he cannot enter into the Kingdom of God. 6That which is born of the flesh is flesh; and that which is born of the Spirit is spirit. 7Marvel not that I said unto thee, Ye must be born again. 8The wind bloweth where it listeth, and thou hearest the sound thereof, but canst not tell whence it cometh, andwhither it goeth: so is every one that is born of the Spirit. 9Nicodemus answered and said unto him, Howcan these things be? 10Jesus answered and said unto him, Art thou a master of Israel, and knowest not these things?11Verily, verily, I say unto thee, We speak that we do know, and testify that we have seen; and ye receive not our witness. 12If I have told you earthly things, and ye believe not, how will ye believe, if I tell you of heavenly things? 13And no man hath ascended up to heaven, but he that came down from heaven, even the Son of man which is in heaven. 14And as Moses lifted up the serpent in the wilderness, even so must the Son of man be lifted up:15That whosoever believeth in him should not perish, but have eternal life. 16For God so loved the world, that he gave his only begotten Son, that whosoever believeth in him should not perish, but have everlasting life (*KJV*, John 3:1-16).

Jesus told Nicodemus that he needed to be born again to

understand all that Jesus taught. Nicodemus was a man who owed his birth to Judaism and obedience to the commandments described in the Law. The way he was reasoning was determined by a Jewish worldview:

- The Gentiles are sinners and the Jews are the light bearers of the world.
- Salvation is deliverance from political oppression.
- Justification comes by obedience to the law.
- Money and blessings are a sign of your obedience to the law.
- The Jews are the people of God.
- Man is the servant of God and can never be at the right hand of God.

The list goes on.

Jesus explained to Nicodemus how he could be born again, and have a brand new foundation from where God's reasoning could give birth to a new life in him. He explained that the Son of Man (the representative of mankind in their sin, and as a man under the law, representing the law) had to be lifted up as the snake was lifted up in the desert (See Num. 21:4-8). He went on to explain that those who believe in what actually happened in the Son of Man when He was crucified, as the LAW man and the SIN man, will be saved.

The snake represented the **doctrine of the devil**—the satanic system of legalism and works righteousness—in which a person sees good works as the only way to have eternal life. A new birth would be to see the law system, and the death it brought, die on the pole just as the people lived when they looked at the snake dying on the pole (See

Num. 21).

Similarly, when you see Jesus, a man under the law—representing the law-man and carrying all sin of all people—dying on the cross, and see that in His death you are no longer under the law nor are you a sinner anymore, you receive the new birth! All who can see Jesus on the cross have come to the conclusion that the law is not the light of the world and that man stands forgiven of all sin. Having this conclusion as the foundation of your thinking opens your eyes to the Kingdom of God. You are now open to the relationship way of doing things, which is portrayed in Elohim (The Divine Ones). As we see this death, we find a new logic and enter into a new platform of reasoning. From this platform, we can understand the Kingdom of God and even enter into its power. We will no longer owe our financial standing to the law and willpower. The power derived from our newfound reality, which is based in truth, will be the source of our new life.

It will be impossible for us to seek the Kingdom of God and His righteousness, if we are still clinging to the concept of traditional "financial principles." As long as we cannot see the sowing and reaping system and tithing crucified— lifted up as the snake was lifted up in the desert—it will be impossible to see or enter the Kingdom of God in the area of finances. Unless the foundation of our reasoning concerning money is born again, by seeing those law systems lifted up as the snake was in the desert, we will not understand or experience what Jesus was talking about in the 6th chapter of Matthew:

33But seek ye first the Kingdom of God, and his

righteousness; and all these things will be added unto you.[34]*Take therefore no thought for the morrow: for the morrow will take thought for the things of itself. Sufficient unto the day is the evil thereof* (*KJV*, Matt. 6:33, 34).

CHAPTER 8

God intended life

This introduction to Chapter 8 is from Brennan Manning's audio message, *The Relentless Tenderness of Jesus*. It is essential for you to read this to better understand my message:

An old Hasidic rabbi, from the Ukraine, claimed that he learned the meaning of love from a drunken peasant. One morning the rabbi was out in the Polish countryside to visit a friend of his who owned a tavern. When the rabbi walked in, he saw two men seated at a table who were gloriously in their cups, drunk as skunks, stoned out of their minds, arms wrapped around each other, each guy reassuring the other one how much he loved him.

Suddenly Ivan said to Peter, 'Peter, tell me what hurts me.' Blurry eyed, Peter said, 'How do I know what hurts you?'
Ivan's answer was swift... 'If you don't know what hurts me, how could you say you love me? 'What made Jesus Christ the greatest Lover in human history is that He really knew, and He knows today, what is hurting His people. Back in 1981, a friend of mine, an Episcopal priest in Columbus,

Ohio, walked into his office on a Monday morning, wrote a hasty letter of resignation to the vestry and then he returned to his home and sat down at the kitchen table and wrote a letter to his wife and three children, all of the kids under the age of ten, that he was abandoning them.

He fled to a logging camp in New England and took on a job as a logger. One Saturday afternoon in January, when it was ten degrees below zero, this priest was sitting in a portable, aluminium trailer that he had rented. The only source of heat was a tiny portable, aluminium heater. Well, the heater suddenly quit and died and within minutes the temperature in the trailer was below zero. Shivering, in a fit of rage, the priest picked up the heater and flung it through the window, broke the window, and shouted, 'Christ, I hate you! Damn it, God, get out of my life! I'm finished with this Christian crap! It's all over!' He sank to his knees, defeated and weeping.

In the midst of his hopelessness, he heard a voice from within say, 'It's okay, Kevin. I understand, and I'm here. I'm with you, and I'm for you.' And then he heard Jesus weeping within him. Christ felt what he was feeling. It was an overwhelming experience of intimacy.

That same afternoon Kevin Martin packed his bags and returned to Columbus to be reconciled with his family and his church and has gone on to pastor the most dynamic, spiritually alive Episcopal church in America - St. Luke's in Seattle, Washington.

'Here is my servant, whom I have chosen, my Beloved, the favourite of my soul and He will proclaim the true faith to the nations. The bruised reed He will not crush. The

smouldering wick, He will not quench' (Isaiah 42:1-3). If you read the gospel closely, you will notice how fine-tuned Jesus is to our anger, our frustration, our emptiness, our loneliness, our fears, our self-hatred, our shame. Throughout His public ministry on earth—the encounter with the prostitute in the time of the Pharisees, the adulteress woman in the age of stoning, the thrice denying Peter when He was denied, and the young apostle John in the upper room on the night before He died, here we capture the essence of the life of Jesus.

The Greek verb, splagchnizomai, is used twelve times in the four gospels and is usually translated to English as, 'He was moved with compassion.' However, because of the poverty of our English vocabulary, we really don't capture the deep meaning of splagchnizomai, so depending on the translation of the bible you use, it may say, 'He was moved with pity, or He felt sorry for them, or His heart went out to them.' But again, they missed the profound physical and emotional flavour of this Greek verb, splagchnizomai which is derived from the noun, splagma, meaning, the bowels, (entrails, intestines), the deepest parts of a person from which the strongest emotions, like love and hatred, arrive.

We must never forget that when we speak of the compassion of Jesus, we are speaking of the compassion of the infinite, transcendent, Almighty God of the sacred Man, defined by the Council of Nicaea in the year 325 AD, as being co-equal and consubstantial to the Father, God from God, Light from Light, True God from True God.

The compassion of Jesus is the compassion of God Himself and Jesus says to your heart and mine, 'Don't ever be so foolish as to measure my compassion for you in terms of your compassion for one another. Don't ever be so silly as to compare your thin, pallid, wavering, capricious, fickle, moody, dependent on human circumstances, human compassion with mine, for I am God as well as Man.' What I'm driving at is this: When you read the gospels, that Jesus was moved with compassion, it is saying His gut was wrenched, His heart torn open, the most vulnerable part of His being lay bare.

Splagchnizomai, in Greek, is related to the Hebrew word for compassion, rachamim, which refers to the womb of Yahweh.

Compassion is such a deep, central, powerful emotion in Jesus Christ, that it can only be described as a movement within the womb of God Himself, where all of divine tenderness and gentleness lie hidden, where God is Mother, Father, Brother, Sister, Son and Daughter, who all feel the emotions, and passions are one in divine love.

The numerous physical healings performed by Jesus, and recorded in the gospels, are only a hint of the anguish in the heart of God's Son toward all humanity. Even the passion and death of Jesus on Calvary is only a hint of His deep compassion, and the substance of our faith lies in the conviction that beyond that hint lay compassion and love beyond measure.

When Jesus was moved with compassion, when He wept within the brokenness of my friend, Kevin Martin, the gospel is saying: 'The ground of all being shook, the Source of all life trembled, the heart of all love burst open and the unfathomable depth of the relentless tenderness was laid bare. — Brennan Manning (Taken from a message called – Relentless Tenderness – preached not long before he died. https://www.youtube.com/watch?v=EK4hNCxutkg)

When I think of the compassion of God and hear what Brennan Manning said in his study of the Greek and Hebrew, it just boggles my mind! The relentless tenderness of God towards man is wonderful beyond expression! To think that the very womb of God—the very source that keeps everything in its place—starts to move, ready to bring forth and manifest His life in us. I listened to the audio of Brennan Manning maybe a hundred times, and every time I listen to it I want to cry because I think of this awesome, wonderful God who has such a high quality of life that He can find His very being moved by what others are experiencing. He is a God that is not distant but close to His people. He feels what they feel. He has such liberation about Him that He thinks of others more than Himself. He is a being that is so flooded with life, and the kind of life He possesses is such that He cannot live outside of seeing others experiencing that life. That is the God with whom we have to do.

We don't sit with a God who is on the other side of space and time, peering at us through a little window in a box, a box where we are trying to live a good enough life for Him to smile over us. He is a God who is very intimately involved with us. He is a God who is not interested in giving rules but in sharing His life with us. He wants to indwell us so that He can make His emotions, and His passions—and the love from where it all flows—available to us. To God, it is worthless for people to be acting right, while not sharing in the same platform from where His love and life are born. It would be like taking a friend, who is not a fisherman at heart, on a fishing trip with you. He can only go through the motions because his heart is not in it. Because of who God is, we are exposed to the highest quality of life in the One who knows what hurts us and what makes us happy.

I like what Brennan's friend heard after he threw the heater out the window: Jesus said within him, "*It's okay, Kevin. I understand, and I'm here. I'm with you, and I'm for you.*" What touches me the most is that he heard Jesus weeping **inside** of him. It wasn't an outside weeping in disappointment: "You have failed again!" It was an inside weeping of compassion, for He was feeling what this priest was feeling, even when he was so frustrated that he was screaming at God, "Get out of my life!"

I am reminded of a teaching I taught many years ago about the word *mercy*. The word "mercy" means *deeds of compassion that flow from the innermost being, the core or the spine of somebody, with a purpose to treat another person better than what he would ever deserve according to the law.*

Mercy and compassion are so intertwined that we cannot separate these things from each other. We need to understand that we are dealing with a God who reveals to Moses that He is merciful (See Exodus 33). He is a God who, in His innermost being, feels what we feel. It's not that He sort of has an idea about how we're feeling. No! The very feeling you feel is what He feels. That is the compassion of the Divine Ones; they want to be known by it, and freely give us access to their heart of compassion. The access is not only for us, in receiving His compassion, but also in knowing what it feels like to have it live in us and compel us to feel compassion for others.

As powerful as this message by Brennan Manning is, as I heard it, there was something that broke my heart. He said, "Never compare human compassion with the compassion of the Almighty." I understand what he was trying to say, but when I heard this, I had an eternal no rise up in my heart. I said, "This is not right! This is not the way it's supposed to be! God, how can you exclude us from having that quality of life? I'm not settling for that! I'm not settling for a life where the very compassion of God is not born into my heart." The end goal that God has with man is to **live** in us, **feel** in us, and **will** in us from our perfect oneness with Him.

What a sad day it would be, if we were so conditioned by religion that all our lives amounted to was the material things God had given us, instead of sharing in His very life, living with Him and like Him, in a place where He lives in and through us!

I have never understood what it means when the Bible says that it is "**more blessed to give than to receive**" (See Acts 20:35). That verse was shoved down our throats as some kind of spiritual—and usually financial—thing. It was only as I came to understand Elohim sharing their Trinity life with human beings that this verse made sense for the very first time. Once the understanding of the Trinity and our design becomes the foundation from where we reason, it all becomes so clear.

Let me use an example to explain why only in our Oneness with the Trinity is it more blessed to give than to receive:

A lion in a cage can receive food and help from a person who has compassion on him to free him from the cage. Yet, this compassion is a feeling no lion has for people who are locked up in jail. This is why the life of an animal is just not as blessed as the life of a human. While it is a blessing for man or beast to receive freedom, when you co-live with God, sharing in the way He lives, you enter the highest life that can be attained.

To experience God's very emotions compelling you is the "more blessed," from Acts 20:35. What's "more blessed" is to have been set free, rather than being in need of freedom, and to have the Saviour's heart born in you to the point of setting others free. Having real life—the God intended life—is all about Him living in and through us, by the perfect union that is in Elohim (the Divine Ones).

Compassion in Persecution

I have experienced, first hand, what bible schools teach, and most of them warn their students never to teach on money because it is such a sensitive topic. Helena and I have had many churches reject our ministry because of what we believe and boldly proclaim. We have received so much persecution that some of the biggest ministries have kicked me out for saying what you hear me teach in this book. When I stand in that persecution, I feel lonely and I feel like it's basically only me preaching this. When you think of the turmoil you can put your family through by preaching this, you feel alone! Yet, in the midst of all the persecution, the comfort of this compassionate God who loves me is awesome. He's wonderful!

When we know that He feels with us, and we hear Him

inside us saying, "It's okay," it blesses and inspires us. It is so blessed to be the recipient of Elohim's compassion that it compels us to continue to preach boldly with extravagant love, even to those who are against us. It is a life we could never attain apart from walking in the light of what He's done for us. It is tangible and liberating; it's what we've always wanted!

In all the years of being persecuted, I've come to learn that it is even more blessed to feel compassion towards others—even our persecutors—than to be on the receiving end of God's compassion. It is the highest quality of life to be experienced, a logic that is wider than your own circumstances and financial well-being. It's thrilling to experience God living His life in you, where your gut is torn for others' pain and you can feel their joy. It's wonderful to be at a place where the revelation of the value of others brings you to say, "I am not overly anxious about my own well-being anymore."

Life is truly experienced when the zeal that God has for people consumes us. Fortunately, God has not excluded us from feeling what it's like to love others, by only making us the recipients of love. As we enter the place of Elohim relationship in the Trinity, based on our union with God by the fact that there is a human being in the Godhead, we receive the life of God. We feel loved and we start to love by an inner power that we never knew.

How could we, as the Church, sit at a place where we settle for mediocre compassion and a mediocre life, when the Trinitarian life of God has been made available to us? God's very nature is compassion. God's very nature is love. But, His end goal wasn't just for you to experience His compassion in the form of receiving compassion. His end goal was for you to experience what it is to BE compassionate and so live forever with Him. That is the highest quality of life that there is. That is what He enjoys and has come to bring to us and that is what eternal life is all about. Let's never settle for the kind of life where we are cursed to only live by a human compassion and human generosity, when the grace of God has been made available for us.

When God made man, His ultimate purpose was for man to share in the quality of life that He possesses—not to have a mediocre life compared to His life! Compassion is not just something that flows when it goes bad with somebody. When compassion is the strong link between two parties, the one is so much a part of the other one that he shares also in his joys. It is an absolute union where liberation from a life of selfishness takes place. This is where our thoughts expand beyond ourselves. This is the compassionate life the Trinity has possessed for all eternity. It is the very life of God which is now accessible to us! When God made man, He **made us to partake of His life.** The Father lives in absolute compassion and union with Jesus and He created man to also have that life. AND THAT IS CALLED **GRACE!**

"The LORD is gracious, and full of compassion; slow to anger, and of great mercy" (*KJV*, Ps. 145:8).

It Can Only Come by God Infusing His Life into You

Religious teachings on sowing and reaping, the famous teaching on tithing where you always owe God, and the promises of having more will never bring us to the place where we can experience God's life of compassion and generosity. Never! By rules and regulations, no person will be justified to have true life (See Rom. 3:20, Gal. 2:16). God's plan was to have man as a being who can feel what it's like to be like Him. By legalism, man will never know how it feels to be like God. God knows it is impossible for man to have that heart, and that call and passion, by working to keep some commandments or principles. It can only come by God infusing His life into you. Based onour design, it can only manifest in us when we are **persuaded of the truth**, revealed to us in the incarnation death and resurrection of Jesus, and now sitting in the Godhead as a human, being the very place he has prepared for us all.

It would be legalistic to say, "God is the God who gives, therefore, I must give." No! God is the God who has "giving" in His mind, because He is moved with compassion. So, **LET** Him be compassionate to you, by opening your heart to Him saying, "God, not only am I receiving the compassion that You have in Your heart *for* me, but I am even receiving Your compassion to the point that it can manifest **in** me. My life is made available for me to **co-experience your life of compassion for others**, as a result of the wonderful union between us that you've provided in Jesus."

Believer, since you are co-seated with Christ in Heaven, and He can feel every sad feeling that is in you, I want to tell you this: Don't be robbed from the truth that it goes both ways! You can also feel and experience the very gut-moving power that is in the Almighty and God's emotion can drive your life! That is what Paul was saying in 2 Corinthians 5:14: "The love of Christ compels us for we are of this mind: if One died then all are dead" (AMP). When we are of the same mind as the Father, seeing how we have been unified in Christ's death, we find the life of the Divine Ones effortlessly born into us. This is what Paul calls the power that **compels** him.

If we preach that people should do good actions, like giving, yet it isn't born in them from a belief in what He has done in Jesus, where all are forgiven—a birth of love and of that union in the Trinity where He lives in you—it will mean nothing, for it is not His kind of life. **His life is not fuelled by an external commandment but by who He is inside people.** Even if you give your body to be burned for the spreading of the gospel, you are STILL nothing if it is done from the perspective of obedience to a commandment (See 1 Cor. 13:3). Your very being is determined and defined, not by what you do but by what drives you.

We need to be careful; it is not a wilful decision that love is going to drive us that will give us life. True life manifests in us when the goodness of God consumes our very belief and the core of our being. All we need is to be listening to the message of His love and grace, found in the perfect oneness between God and man, in Jesus. Since the moment the MAN Jesus was raised from the dead, and sat down at the right hand of the Father, we have had **access** to all of God's life, person, and way of living.

We are Not Hopelessly Trying to Copy the Life of Jesus

We have come to Mt. Zion; we have come to the city of the living God; we have come to the place where God says, "I indwell my people." We have not come to the mountain that smokes with the glory cloud of the law (See Heb. 12:18-24). We have not come to a place where we observe outside commandments we must try to obey, hopelessly trying to **copy** the life of Jesus. No! I submit to you that we have come to the place where God—the very being of God—is placed inside you, infused into you! Our union with Him can be likened to a fusion of two metals becoming one, so that we cannot define the difference between the two anymore. When we see and believe His love, we are born from it; a new kind of a being comes into existence.

Steven was not hallucinating, when while being stoned, he cried out, *"Look! I see the heavens opened and the Son of Man standing at the right hand of God!"* (NKJV, Acts 7:56). He didn't just say, "I see *Jesus* standing at the right hand of God." He said much more than that! He was telling the crowd that **mankind was elevated to the Godhead**: "I see the **Son of MAN** standing at the right hand of God." They killed Steven for saying those words.

The purpose of works is not to gain you points with God. God prepared good works as the way by which we can express His life born into us. If you feel love, you can express love in actions that come naturally to you. If you feel generosity, you can express it in ways that will give full expression to who and what you are. God prepared these good works beforehand so that we could have a place to express His life in us. He did not prepare good works beforehand as a way to earn salvation (See Eph. 2:10). The enemy of all life is the belief that one can only have life by following certain commandments and rules. This is finding the definition of yourself in the fruit the system produces in you, when you obey its commands.

Concerning money, having life by keeping commandments is at the core of the teachings on sowing and reaping, tithing, and the first fruit offering.

At this point, I would like you to first understand our design and how we can be robbed from what God intended for us, through these lies about **giving to be blessed.** I went into some detail, in Chapter 2, on how deadly this legalistic system can be. It is the law, which is the power of sin camouflaged in a teaching that says Christian generosity leads to greater financial blessings, manifesting God's prosperity. And in case there is any confusion, it is also being under the law system to say, "Ok I get it, we don't have to give to be blessed, so now under grace, we GET to give by God empowering us to do so, in order to be blessed" This can still be coming from the *giving to be blessed* system, only in a roundabout way.

Why should the Church settle for something that can never produce life in the area of money? No man-made law can ever produce generosity. Why should we, out of fear of not having for tomorrow, cling to some old system that will rob us from knowing what it feels like to have our innermost being moved with compassion when we see someone in need, or feel our pocket open to make someone else happy? Why? And leaders, why do we always have to keep some back door open for financial provision in the church, through incorporating the tithing, and sowing and reaping, in some form or fashion, when God has a master plan by which man can experience His eternal life and freedom?

The Better Way

In his second letter to the church in Corinth, Paul gives us an example of a church that was experiencing what it's like to live the God-intended life, having no fear at all about money:

1 Moreover, brethren, we do you to wit of the grace of God
bestowed on the churches of Macedonia; 2 How that in a
great trial of affliction the abundance of their joy and
their deep poverty abounded unto the riches of their
liberality. 3 For to their power, I bear record, yea, and
beyond their power they were willing of
themselves; 4 Praying us with much entreaty that we would
receive the gift, and take upon us the fellowship of the
ministering to the saints (*KJV*, 2 Cor. 8:1-4).

What Paul said is written in a very difficult manner. He was trying to say that in the very midst of the Macedonian's deep poverty, he could see their freedom expressed in their liberality, and he was amazed:

Now, friends, I want to report on the surprising and generous ways in which God is working in the churches in Macedonia province. Fierce troubles came down on the people of those churches, pushing them to the very limit. The trial exposed their true colours: They were incredibly happy, though desperately poor. The pressure triggered something totally unexpected: an outpouring of pure and generous gifts. I was there and saw it for myself. They gave offerings of whatever they could—far more than they could afford! —pleading for the privilege of helping out in the relief of poor Christians (*MSG*, 2 Cor. 8:1-4).

This poverty-stricken church got such a divine grace influence on the heart. They were so divinely influenced in their belief, and so liberated concerning fear and money, that they begged the apostles to let them participate in the financial giving to the poor churches in Jerusalem. They said, "Don't rob us from the **joy** of giving to this poor church in Jerusalem!" These people were so under the divine influence of God that their gut was torn with compassion. The relentless tenderness of God, which surpasses all understanding, had such a powerful influence in the poor people of the Macedonian church, that they were liberated. Their minds were so enlarged that they couldn't even see their own need. They said, "Let's share in the **joy** of contributing to someone else!"

This passage is **not** saying that, if we claim to be under grace, we should give with joy and in abundance; that would be a complete abuse of the verse. If we see it from that angle, we have missed the boat, and we are believing something that will kill us! The idea is not to use that as a command, telling people, "You must now give!" The idea is to introduce people to God's grace as the power that fuels His life in them. We see that the people in Macedonia first gave themselves to God. Giving yourself to God is not what we always thought. It is not the giving my life to Jesus message of repentance of sins for salvation. The giving of oneself to God is making yourself available to be engulfed by what was made available in the incarnation, death and resurrection of Jesus Christ, by simply believing the truth it declares. It is your favourable response to God's warm embrace, experienced in His invitation to commune with Him in the Godhead.

The Macedonians gave themselves to God, and they also gave themselves to Paul and the apostles. The dynamics at work in the union they shared with Elohim included

Paul and what he felt like doing for the poor. Both Paul and the poor churches in Macedonia were co-seated with Christ; therefore, they were co-sharing in the compassion that was in the heart of God for the poor in Jerusalem at that moment. Paul experienced the gut wrenching compassion of God for the poor in Jerusalem. The people in Macedonia were open to co-experience it, resulting in a freedom that was not expected. They were liberated to the point that they were free from the fear of not having, becoming completely **blind to their earthly poverty**. The dynamics at work in the heart of Paul and the poor churches of Macedonia is what I call "the transcendent life of Elohim." To me, that is **the New Testament way of giving** and **the only God- intended way of living**.

I'm not changing from this Gospel, for this has set me free! And I'm not settling for stinginess, and I'm not settling for legalism. I am only settling for His quality of life inside my life! The Church is in desperate need of this word in the area of money! It saddens me to see how many preachers—even those who are proclaiming the message of grace pretty accurately—compromise when it comes to the truth on money. By no means do I say that I am better, or more righteous, or have attained to more than any other person or preacher. The love of God for all people floods my heart.

My prayer for my brothers and sisters is that they will be strengthened by the Holy Spirit to boldly declare grace about the greatest bondage on mankind—money! Seeing blessings and prosperity as the friend that seals the deal on joy, peace, salvation, and living in the kingdom will only lead to unending pain and frustration. This is not the life God has dreamed for us to have. I would like to end this chapter by telling two true stories about living in true financial freedom founded in grace:

Are we really poor?

While listening to the radio as I drove from Malmesbury to Cape Town, I heard this true story over the radio: A pastor in a very affluent area announced that they had a poor family in their church to whom they wanted to give some money. They asked their members to give on a regular basis towards a special love donation, so that all of the money could then be given to the family when they had collected a generous amount. Among the people who began to give was a lady who was very eager to contribute and she told her children about it. As a family project, they began to give sacrificially and joyfully. (Sacrificial giving is giving that involves a change of lifestyle to make the giving possible.) The family baked cakes to sell, and even went so far as to switch off their electricity for a few nights in the week to save the money to give to the poor family. On a weekly basis, they turned their earnings from selling the cakes over to the church, and also gave what they had saved monthly by switching off their electricity. After several months of giving, the pastor announced that it was time to give the money to the poor family.

One evening some weeks later, there was a knock at the lady's door; it was the pastor. This was a surprise to the family, since he didn't normally visit them without an appointment. After a friendly conversation about the weather, school, and politics, he handed the lady an envelope and left. It was a check for a large amount of money with a card signed by the members of their congregation: "God loves you and we love you, too!"

The mom turned and asked her children, "Are we poor?"

Her son replied, "We thought we had more than enough. We even gave into this donation. This must be a mistake!"

So, because the "poor" family found it very difficult to use the money, they returned it to the church to be used for someone else. They never knew they were poor at all.

This is such a wonderful example of how blind a person can become to his or her own needs in the presence of true inner wealth.

I don't want diamonds.

(The following is a true story.)

A few days ago, when I stopped to visit one of my friends in a nearby town, he told me that he grew up in the Cullinan area in South Africa, an area known for its large, high quality diamonds. Years after he left Cullinan, a Christian woman discovered a large diamond worth a very large amount of money. Can you imagine the joy that flooded her heart when she found it? It was a large diamond! So large that it meant the end of all debt for the woman and her family—in fact, the end of *all* financial difficulties forever. Of course, this would be a dream come true for anyone.

Before she could cash in the diamond, though, a beggar came to her door, asking for food. She did not feel she wanted to give him food but the diamond; so she followed the passion in her heart and handed the large diamond to the beggar. In great amazement, the beggar quickly ran from her house, hiding the diamond tightly in his hands.

Many years later, the lady heard a knock at the door, and upon opening the door she saw that it was the same beggar she had given the diamond to many years ago. To her amazement, the beggar did not want food or money but reached into his pocket and handed her something. It was the diamond!

“Ma’am, I don’t want this diamond. I want what it was that made you give me the diamond.”

CHAPTER 9

You Can Do All Things

Before I came to the knowledge of the truth, one of the scariest concepts I had to deal with was **being content**, especially in the area of money. Since **contentment** was seen as apathy and being backslidden, if you had sickness, or didn't have a lot of money, or had other troubles, you were obviously consenting to the will of Satan in your life. It wasn't until years later that I realized what I was missing out on in my discontentment. I was actually rejecting the promised progress and success that can only come by His love for me.

Very Hungry People Will Eat Anything You Feed Them

I was one of those preachers who believed that as long as the people were hungry for more, seeking greater miracles and higher revelation, I had a job. Their dissatisfaction and need for more fuelled my ministry, even giving me a reason to exist. I had entered what I call the *hunger system.* The hungrier people are the more food a restaurant can sell. As a matter of fact, very hungry people will eat just about anything you dish up, and they will pay a lot of money for it! If you can keep them hungry, you can keep them under your power. VERY hungry people will eat anything you feed them, even if it is half rotten. I've seen this many times and it is a sad state to be in. But, once you start to experience the life of God living in you, your hunger is over forever!

I would define the *hunger system* as the place where we make use of principles, legalism or any good thing we need to do in order to produce the life of God in our life. The system that says *gain is godliness* is a perfect example of a system that can never satisfy. When will you ever have enough? When will you ever reach the wealth of God? Never! Can you see how this belief will keep you in a place where you will never be content?

On the other hand, we also find in the hunger system, the people who accept poverty. They will reject opportunities for provision and prosperity, sacrificing wealth to live in poverty as if that is holiness. This is also not contentment. Paul was content in times of wealth as well as in times of poverty. Paul learned that the feeling of holiness, acceptance and love God had for him was never measured by his financial state. Paul lived in a place where nothing you could add to him would add anything to him, nor could anything that you took from him make him poor!

While I was under the *hunger for more* part of the **hunger system**, I wasn't able to articulate it as I can now, since I wasn't following it cognitively. I first had to be delivered from the hunger mentality, before I could see where I really was and what was driving me. I thank God this was only for a short time in my life, and before I had reached very many people with my hunger belief system to pollute them with the death that was driving me. Being content was one of the most confusing concepts to me: *How could I ever not want more, if Jesus died to give me more?* I couldn't ever feel satisfied until I saw the proof of what I was believing for manifest in my life. When healing, prosperity, and success was not becoming a reality in my life, I thought something had to be drastically wrong and I felt a powerful longing to correct the error. This is the place where the different voices of Obedience god, Ruler god, Precept god and Kingdom god started, with their ever-increasing instructions, using Scriptures to confirm and fuel my insatiable hunger for proof and manifestation of what I believed.

I Lived in a Perpetual Need for Change

Anything in my life that I believed to be contrary to the full success, defined in Deuteronomy 28, caused the emotion of discontentment, which always left me with the perspective that there is more I must have. I lived in a perpetual need for change. The discontentment born from the "gain is godliness" logic, as I described in Chapter 2, leaves you in a state of mind in which you will do anything—it doesn't matter how radical—to possess what is presumably "available" for you in Jesus, IF you follow the correct principles. It's in that desperate search for help, and any glimmer of hope, that Philippians 4:13 comes in very handy: *"I can do all things through Christ which strengthens me"* (Phil. 4:13). This verse encouraged me that I could indeed push through and do whatever God wanted me to do, in order to have all that He wanted me to have:

Ok, so I can do all things through the strength of Jesus, I can become a person that attains to all the prosperity, gifts and callings God has for me as I obey all the principles. We Christians can take over the world; we can have the biggest businesses and be the most successful people, while living in love. We can establish and advance the kingdom, we can ... we can ... I can ... I can ...

How sad, that my understanding of Philippians 4:13 was completely wrong, and along with other popular scriptural references, was actually used by Satan to drive me to the point of exhaustion. Scripture was even used by Satan to push me to serve him to a certain degree. Like Jesus in the desert, if He had agreed to throw Himself off the temple or make stones into bread, He would have been serving Satan by obeying his commands, backed by Scripture (See Matt. 4:1-11).

What is Contentment?

Contentment is not the acceptance of suffering nor is it your embrace of prosperity. It is to be in a place on account of God indwelling you where you see no need to add anything to your life to be truly happy. This is not something you can fake; it is something that happens to you as you come to understand how perfect you are in Jesus. Some have thought of contentment as a state in which you become like a tramp, happy to suffer for Jesus. Is this really any different than giving up hope of a good life altogether? Thinking the acceptance of suffering is contentment is the furthest thing from the truth!

Against all Jewish and human logic, Paul contends that godliness with contentment is the real gain (See 1Tim. 6:6). He describes contentment as a mystery introduced to him by the Lord, which enabled him to live a stable, victorious life, apart from the Jewish conviction that one gains godly blessedness through obedience to the Law:

10 But I rejoiced in the Lord greatly, that now at the last
your care of me hath flourished again; wherein ye were
also careful, but ye lacked opportunity. 11 Not that I
speak in respect of want: for I have learned, in
whatsoever state I am, to be content. 12 I know both how
to be abased, and I know how to abound: everywhere
and in all things I am instructed both to be full and to be
hungry, both to abound and to suffer need. 13 I can do all
things through Christ which strengthens
me. 14 Notwithstanding ye have well done, that ye did
communicate with my affliction (*KJV*, Phil. 4:10-14).

Verse 10 —Lacking Opportunity

But I rejoiced in the Lord greatly, that now at the last your care of me hath flourished again; wherein ye were also careful, but ye lacked opportunity (*KJV*, Phil. 4:10).

In verse 10, Paul thanks the people for giving to him and caring for him. He also explains that he understands itwas due to a lack of opportunity that it took a long time for them to give. In those days, they lacked the luxury of Western Union or PayPal to transfer money to Paul in a quick and efficient way. They needed an opportunity to send the gift with a traveller to the town where Paul was staying. To get such an opportunity must have taken some time. This verse reveals Paul's heart of gratitude, compassion, and understanding for the church in Philippi.

Verse 11 – Learning to be Content

"Not that I speak in respect of want: for I have learned, in whatsoever state I am, to be ***content"*** (*KJV*, Phil. 4:11).

In verse 11, Paul reveals something that is not very common in church circles today. He says that his conversation with the church in Philippi, and his opinion about their support, was not from the perspective of "want." When we look at Paul's situation, we can see that he was afflicted and in need. He was suffering in poverty and going through a very tough time financially. Yet, in the midst of his trying time, he boldly states that it has no influence on the motive of his heart, conduct, or speech.

What a blessed life, to have this kind of stability even when you are caught in the clutches of deepest poverty. Paul is describing what prosperity really is, in its truest form, and he's giving us the reason why he could live free from his situation being the source of his emotions and thoughts about who he is in the eyes of God. He credits his stable emotions and pure motive to contentment, something he has come to learn in his grace journey.

The word *content* means *to have no need of external proof.* Contentment could also be described as the fruit of a mind at rest because of what the heart believes, seeking no proof of what is already established as truth. Contentment was not Paul's acceptance of suffering nor was it his embrace of prosperity. Contentment is a place where the resurrected Jesus, and what He has done, is the final word and only confirmation we need to live in Elohim reality. It is complete deliverance from the *love of* ... system, as I have described earlier in this book.

Contentment is a life in which the belief that *I am what I do or what I have* is completely eradicated from one's heart. It wasn't that Paul had no needs; he *was* in need, while at the same time having no need for those externals to be met **in order to have peace of mind and heart**. In other words, Paul could have a material need without believing something that would give that need the power to determine who he was and how he should feel. He looked into the law of liberty, the law that states we are perfectly liberated from the system by which external circumstances become our "friend" that seals the deal on our salvation and blessedness.

Verse 12 — Whether Abased or Abounding

I know both how to be abased, and I know how to abound: everywhere and in all things I am instructed both to be full and to be hungry, both to abound and to suffer need (*NKJV*, Phil. 4:12).

In verse 12, Paul says that he knows how to be *abased*, which in the Greek means *to be of very low rank in the eyes of others because of your situation*. It is not possible, by a decision of the will, to be content with others' low opinion of you; it comes only by way of a new belief system, rooted in Jesus as the final Word about you! The same is true when you are *abounding*, which in the Greek means that you *have more than what you need.* Just as Paul would not speak in respect of want while poor, he would not speak in respect of prosperity when rich in the physical world.

It's interesting that Paul tells the Philippians he was **instructed** both to be full and suffer lack. The word *instructed,* according to the Greek, means that he was *introduced to the mystery of enjoying a stable life that cannot be adversely affected by having little or having much*! We can clearly see that contentment was a mystery, something that was hidden to the world but now revealed.

Verse 13 — Comes from Jesus

"I can do all things through Christ which strengthens me" (*NKJV*, Phil. 4:13).

In verse 13, we can now understand the true context of what Paul is getting at, when he applauds the message of Christ, for enabling him to be free from the legalistic *love of*… system, where acceptance and success is defined by material wealth. *I can do all things through Christ* has nothing to do with getting rich.

Verse 13 is remarkable in that it shows how Paul fully understood the Gospel and how Christ enables us to have joy, whether we are **in poverty or prosperity**. Paul was not saying that Jesus came in and supernaturally rescued him from his poverty; but in the midst of his poverty, Jesus gave him the ability to have a high quality of life so that neither prosperity nor poverty could determine his emotions and actions. Paul found the inner strength of contentment by believing Jesus is the Messiah.

As we are persuaded of Jesus' impact on the human race, we find that contentment comes **effortlessly** to our hearts. It is a fruit of knowing and believing in what Christ's work at the cross, and His resurrection, has accomplished for all people. It's important to understand that we cannot fake contentment. It is not something we can develop within ourselves by simply deciding we want it; having a great desire for it does not provide enough power to bring it forth. Contentment is a fruit of believing in the end of the law system. It is the natural outcome of believing in the fulfillment of the law and your union in the Trinity, because of the incarnation of God into human flesh.

Verse 10 and 14—With Paul in his Affliction

I'm glad in God, far happier than you would ever guess—happy that you're again showing such strong concern for me (*MSG*, Phil. 4:10).

"Notwithstanding ye have well done, that ye did communicate with my affliction" (*KJV*, Phil. 4:14).

I don't mean that your help didn't mean a lot to me—it did. It was a beautiful thing that you came alongside me in my troubles (*MSG*, Phil. 4:14).

From the Message Bible we can see what Paul is saying:

Not that you ever quit praying and thinking about me; you just had no chance to show it. Actually, I don't have a sense of needing anything, personally. I've learned, by now, to be quite content whatever my circumstances. I'm just as happy with little as with much, and with much as with little. I've found the recipe for being happy, whether full or hungry, hands full or hands empty. Whatever I have, wherever I am, I can make it through anything in the One who makes me who I am. I don't mean that your help didn't mean a lot to me—it did! It was a beautiful thing that you came alongside me in my troubles (*MSG*, Phil. 4:10-14).

In verse 14, we can see that contented Paul received

provision from people and he was grateful for it. Contentment does not mean that we cannot expect God to provide for us. Paul makes it clear that being happy in the midst of your poverty does not mean God will not provide for you materially. It's clear that God did provide for Paul, and He promises that He will care for us as well. Paul was resting in God's love for him, not *faithing* for a change, but believing in the goodness and love of his Father. Paul was completely at peace that everything he needed, as mentioned by Jesus in Matthew 6:33, would be added to him.

In summary of Philippians 4:10-14, contentment is the foundation from where we can live *while* God meets our needs. Contentment is not the acceptance of poverty. It's enjoying life *as* God cares for you, and the how, what, and when of His care for you has no bearing on your acceptance, relationship, or obedience to Elohim.

Let's also look at verse 19 in Philippians 4:

"But my God shall supply all your need according to his riches in glory by Christ Jesus" (*KJV*, Phil. 4:19).

Philippians 4:19 takes on new meaning in the light of what Paul stated in the previous verses. If you feel the need to have external proof of who you are, by having an external need met, you are falling for the same trick Satan tried on Jesus in the desert (See Matt. 4:1-11). By appealing to what Satan saw as Jesus' internal need to have proof of His sonship, Satan challenged Him to use His power to change external situations: command these stones become bread, or throw yourself down from the temple. What we all need is to be internally need-free, free from the need for external proof of who we are in relation to God. Even if you are in need of contentment, it can be met by God. Let contentment be the first need God meets in your life!

He is with you all the time.

5Let your conversation be without covetousness; and be content with such things as ye have: for he hath said, "I will never leave thee, nor forsake thee." 6So we may boldly say: "The Lord is my helper; I will not fear. What can man do to me? (*NKJV*, Heb. 13:5, 6).

I have found the best way to explain a verse is to translate it into what I see in it. Here is the Bertie Brits translation of Hebrews 13:5, 6:

5Allow the life in you to manifest for what it truly is, a life that is not based on money being the friend that seals the deal on your union and togetherness with God, as we as Jews so loved to believe. Since God has boldly declared that He will never leave you nor forsake you, external conformation of His togetherness with us has lost its voice. 6God helps us all the time in providing contentment as well as meeting everyday needs. This makes us fearless, for even the fear of losing all our possessions in persecution cannot influence our decisions, for it has no bearing on our lives. (Bertie Brits)

To me, this kind of life is all I ever wanted. What a blessed life, based on extreme inner wealth!

There *is* financial gain for us.

"But godliness with contentment is great ***gain****"* (*KJV*, 1 Tim. 6:6).

Godliness with contentment is great gain. The word *gain,* in this verse, is directly connected to *money* in the Greek, which means *money-getting,* or simply **getting money**. I have seen many people who do business from a platform of contentment, making much wiser decisions than those who chase after the more. Those who do business from a platform of **discontentment** and chasing after riches, pierce themselves through with many sorrows, always overworking themselves, never having time for their families, having ulcers, needing sleeping pills and having panic attacks. While a lot of those people do increase in earthly wealth, they do so at the cost of peace! This is not what God had in mind for us. He wants us to always be content. Any form of financial gain, which is also accompanied by peace, comes from a content heart.

Let me share a practical experience from my own life about contentment. Two days ago, a friend who loves me asked if I would like to buy his SUV at a very low price. The car is in very good condition and would really be nice to have. I took the car for a test drive and told the man that I will buy it, but need to talk to Helena about it and would have a definite answer for him the next day. As I was thinking about it, I did not feel a need for another car, at the foundation from where I reason; I do not feel I must have a newer car to feel blessed, or feel a need to impress anyone. I already own a car that drives very well. Even if it does have 360,000km on the clock (about 224k miles), it doesn't make sense to go into debt to buy another one.

Since there is no such thing as a deal of a lifetime—it's

now or never ever again—I know that I will get one at a good price again in the future when I want another one. Without feeling in any way that I was losing out, I told my friend that I did not want to buy the car, thanked him for first thinking of me and that was it. I can say, as I sit here, that I have so much peace about the situation. It is very difficult to fall for something that will harm you and your business if you are content!

You can see from this story that godliness with contentment is also the key to having wisdom with your money. Now I can buy all my airline tickets for my upcoming trip to the United States and be under no pressure whatsoever. I am not going to have a single minute of stress over a car payment at all. I am sure I will have another SUV some time and be very impressed by how God provides it for me. And if I never drive one after the one I now have, so what? This is the mystery of **contentment**.

Let's first read 1Tim. 6:6-10 in the NKJV, then I will translate it into what I believe it says:

6 *But godliness with contentment is great gain.* 7 *For we*
brought nothing into this world, and it is certain we can
carry nothing out. 8 *And having food and raiment let's be*
therewith content. 9 *But they that will be rich fall into*
temptation and a snare, and into many foolish and hurtful
lusts, which drown men in destruction and perdition.
10 *For the love of money is the root of all evil: which while*
some coveted after, they have erred from the faith, and
pierced themselves through with many sorrows (*KJV*,
1Tim. 6:6-10).

Bertie Brits' Interpretation:

A godly life, accompanied by no need for external, financial confirmation of your godliness, as the Jewish culture dictates, is the best place to be when it comes to money and prosperity (1Tim. 6:6).

Since material things are not from everlasting to everlasting, don't give it power to judge and have authority in eternal things (1Tim. 6:7).

Even at a place where you have only food and clothes, don't allow your heart to seek the Jewish external-confirmation system with which these false teachers want to pollute you. Don't have money as the friend that seals the deal on who you are in Him (1Tim. 6:8).

If you give money the voice it always had under the old covenant, your desire to have more will cause you to suffer greatly. You will be tempted by all kinds of desires you did not even imagine, which will lead only to frustration and destruction in your life (1Tim. 6:9).

When money is the friend that seals the deal for you on your acceptance, holiness and righteousness, your heart will be pierced through by one conclusion upon the other, spelling your disqualification. When will enough be enough to give you the final yes on your holiness and acceptance? (1Tim. 6:10).

Thanks be to God that Jesus sealed the deal on our salvation, so that we can now freely enjoy God's life in the here and now! If you take nothing else from Part 1, except this one mighty truth, you are right where God wants you. Once the enemy law system has its foot in the door, with even the slightest thing you must do so that God will do for you, then it's got you where it can bring all kinds of trouble your way. Worst of all, if you are convinced that you must do anything to be blessed by God, instead of the blessing you hope for, you will long for God and even begin to resent Him for not honoring what you are giving for Him.

Because of Jesus, we lack nothing; we are already one with the Father and seated in Heavenly places, blessed with every blessing imaginable. People who come to God with money to buy His acceptance and provision are missing it. They're missing who God really is, what Jesus has already done for all people, and how much God has already provided everything we could ever want or even imagine because He loves us.

The idea that we lack is from Satan; it's what he convinced Adam and Eve of, when they stood in the place of complete acceptance and provision from God. Satan is still working today to convince people they lack, by teaching that they must do something or give a certain amount of their money to ensure their well-being. This is the message that keeps people feeling frustrated and very far from their loving Father. It causes deep insecurity and fear, because we were never meant to pull our own weight with God. He created us to be recipients of His life. He is not a merchant we must pay in order to receive his services!

Jesus served *us* in His death and resurrection. Receive what He has done for you and be free from every obligation to pay your way through life. How can you feel indebted to God and freely loved by Him at the same time? As I said earlier, God is pulling your wagon so just relax in His love and let Him give to you everything Jesus has already purchased through the cross. In this, we lack nothing and we are indebted to no one. We are free from every obligation to muster up anything from ourselves and our resources to get what we feel we need from God.

PART 2

A Dogmatic Look at Traditional Teaching on Money

Introduction

In this part of the book, we are going to critique the traditional and modern interpretations of most scriptures commonly used to support tithing and sowing and reaping. The main purpose of Part 2 is to help those who agree with what I say in Part 1 to have scriptural backing for what they now believe. I am sure that you will say yes to the concepts discussed in Part 1, but your heart will be searching for scriptural confirmation. You can probably already hear all the *yes, but what about this verse and that verse* counter arguments to what we know make family sense. Although this section might seem very technical and analytical, it will be of great value in quieting all the contradicting traditional and modern arguments that still give credence to what we now know cannot be correct.

Anything we teach should be congruent with the Gospel

of Jesus. All modern-day teachings about tithing, in regard to financial giving, are not in line with the Gospel of His grace, since their origin is the system of what we need to do to get God to do something for us or what we owe God. They also have the system of beholding God, and following what we behold in God, as the foundation from where one's blessedness is produced. Let me explain this: Since the Gospel of Jesus Christ is not a message that is founded on what we need to do for God, in order for Him to bless us, there is no room for tithing when we talk about financial contribution in the Gospel message.

Tithing, sowing and reaping, and many of the modern-day teachings on finances, are built on the law of sin and death. I will say, most of those who teach it do so ignorantly, and are not aware of what they are actually saying, and affirming, by teaching it. When we have a look at the Tree of the Knowledge of Good and Evil (referred to as *TOGE*), we will find the basic **system of death** described in its finest detail:

But of the tree of the knowledge of good and evil, thou shalt not eat of it: for in the day that thou eatest thereof thou shalt surely die (*KJV*, Gen. 2:17).

Let's define the Tree of the Knowledge of Good and Evil (TOGE):

I would like you to see that this is not two trees but one tree, the Tree of the Knowledge of **GOOD** and **EVIL**. If you EAT of this tree, you will die:

- *Good* - Who is Good but God? There is only one that is good and it is God (See Mark 10:18).

- *Evil* - In the Greek, it refers to *hard labor and to be flooded with work.*
- *Eat* - When we eat the flesh of Jesus, we believe in His flesh unto life. When we believe in what He has done through His blood, we actually drink His blood. In the same way, you will be eating of the Tree of the Knowledge of Good and Evil when you believe what it states.

God warned Adam that he was not to EAT (believe) that he can look at God (the GOOD) and then work (EVIL) that good, thinking it will feed him. It's one thing to behold God and how He lives, but the moment we try to jot His goodness down into basic principles and rules for us to follow, so that we can have life, we will die. The good life of God can only be reached by Him freely giving it to us. Trying to do the good only God can do will kill you. We even see Paul calling the Ten Commandments the *power of sin* and the *ministration of death*:

"The sting of death is sin, and the **strength of sin is the law**" (*NKJV*, 1 Cor. 15:56).

6Who also made us sufficient as ministers of the new covenant, not of the letter but of the Spirit; for the letter
kills, but the Spirit gives life. 7But if the ministry of death, written and engraved on stones, was glorious, so that the children of Israel could not look steadily at the face of Moses because of the glory of his countenance, which
glory was passing away, 8how will the ministry of the Spirit not be more glorious? (*NKJV*, 2 Cor. 3:6-8).

Something beautiful for the eye, desirable to make you

wise, and flooded with the promise of life—if it could be obeyed—is called *deadly* by God and Paul. God said it first to Adam, and in the New Testament, Paul echoed the word God had spoken to Adam. If we were to take God and break all He is down into principles of life, we would conclude that God loves, God gives; He is kind, merciful, flooded with compassion and keeps no score of evil. But, the moment we behold the beauty of God, broken down into presumably doable small chunks of truth, and try to do them, we will die. The good will be too much for us to do and it will kill us. This is not because good is deadly but on account of design. We have not been designed to find life by what we do, but to be the recipients of life on account of what God does. What God does best is to love.

Unfortunately, we have done exactly that when it comes to money and the church. We beheld the goodness of God and His generosity towards man, jotted His generosity down, then thought that we could have financial prosperity and life by working all the principles of generosity seen between Jesus and people when He walked the earth. All the good the Law commanded is basically God in written format.

Imagine a truck driver, who is not a chef at all and does not even have a passion for cooking, going to the top chef in the world and jotting down all the top chef does, to the finest detail, thinking he will be the best chef by simply following all the principles the top chef follows. Everyone will tell him that cooking will destroy him. Being a good chef is not accomplished by following principles; it is something that comes from the inside.

Jesus came to end the system that Adam implemented, of

looking at the GOOD in GOD, jotting it down in principle form and trying to do it to have life. You might say, "But God gave the LAW, did He not?" Yes, God gave the people what they asked for. Hear what I am saying clearly, He gave them what they asked for, not what He wanted them to have from the beginning. The original plan that God had was not that we have life by doing the things God does. He wanted us to have life by Him doing what He does best, which is to love.

He came to give you life and life on account of Him being good to you. You might be so afraid to hear me talk about *giving* this way. You might even be feeling that your world is falling apart right now. Tithing might be all that you have known for all your life. Sowing and reaping might have been the only hope you've had for the future, and now it is shaken to the core.

I would like to encourage you to keep on reading. Let the love of God reprogram your heart to the point that neither tithing nor any other form of giving, on our part, is the foundation of a stable future, but rather Jesus and what He has done for us in His death and resurrection. This can be difficult for you, but I would like you to rest in His love as He takes you on this journey to true freedom.

As a pastor of a church, you might find this message extremely difficult to stomach, since your financial future could be shaken to its core. You might even think this book is going to bring devastation to your church, so you need to warn as many people as possible about it. I would like to encourage you that there are many others who have walked this path before you.

God is Pulling Your Wagon

Please know that God will never leave you nor forsake you; He is the one caring for you. The Gospel is a *God* story, not a *You and What You Do for Him* story. God is pulling your wagon; just relax in His love. Let God perform the heart operation, removing all that is not from Him, and *He* will bring forth His life in you.

Arguments to be discussed in the second part of this book are as follows:

Tithing

- **The Tithe of Abraham as the New Testament Tithe**

It seems to be common knowledge that Abraham tithed before the Ten Commandments were given. But, the fact that he tithed before the giving of the Law is then used as a foundation from where tithing in the New Testament is preached. The basic reasoning is that everything prior to the giving of the Law is not subject to the fulfillment of the Law, making tithing a valid New Testament principle, because it first occurred before the Law was given in written format. I will explain that this cannot be used as a foundation from where we tithe, based on the historical context in which Abraham tithed.

- **The Levitical Tithe**

It is believed that the Levitical tithe was brought over into the church system as a basic foundation from where tithing in the New Testament should take place. In this part of the book, we test the logic and see that it would be impossible to be done in the New Testament. I will also explain that the Levitical tithe had nothing to do with money at all.

- **The New Testament Tithe of Gratitude in Acknowledgement that Jesus is Risen**
- **Sowing and reaping**

The Foundation for Our Study

Hermeneutics is the study of the methodological principles of Bible interpretation. Exegesis and eisegesis are two conflicting hermeneutical approaches to Bible study:

Exegesis is the exposition, or explanation, of Scripture based on a careful, objective analysis, which is almost impossible to do since all people have preconceived ideas about everything. The word exegesis literally means "to lead **out of**." This is when the interpreter comes to all conclusions by following the text.

Eisegesis is the opposite approach to Scripture, in which the interpretation of a passage is based on a subjective, non-analytical reading. The word eisegesis literally means "to lead **into**." This is when the interpreter injects his own ideas into the text, making it mean whatever he believes or wants it to mean, based on what he has learned in the past, how he personally feels about the subject, mixed with what he has found in his studies or from other sources.

Obviously, only exegesis does justice to the Scriptures as it respects the grammar, syntax, and setting of the text to discover its true meaning. Eisegesis is a mishandling of the text and often leads to misinterpretation. Eisegesis is concerned only with making a point. It is part of our human makeup to have an eisegetical approach to all things. With this in mind, we should always know that eisegetical interpretation of verses is very difficult to avoid, on account of the critical factor in the brain always wanting to affirm what it already believes. The reason I say this is to help you understand that people who have had an eisegetical approach to money scriptures are not willfully trying to mislead others or themselves. On the other hand, 2 Timothy 2:15 commands us to use exegetical methods, which I believe is possible by the power of the Holy Spirit:

Present yourself to God as one approved, a workman who does not need to be ashamed and who correctly handles (rightly divides, correctly expounds on, or interprets) the word of truth (*NKJV*, 2 Tim 2:15).

An honest student of the Bible will be an **exegete** (an **expounder** or textual interpreter), allowing the text to speak for itself. Eisegesis easily lends itself to error, as the would-be interpreter attempts to align the text with his own preconceived notions.

Exegesis allows us to agree with the Bible. Eisegesis seeks to force the Bible to agree with us. The process of **exegesis** involves the following:

- Observation: what does the passage say?
- Interpretation: what does the passage mean?

- Correlation: how does the passage relate to the rest of the Bible? How does what I see in the verse pertain to the death and resurrection of Jesus?
- How does the passage line up with the manifested truth in Jesus when He walked the earth?

Application: how does this passage affect my life?

Eisegesis, on the other hand, involves something quite different:

- Imagination: what idea do I want to present?
- Exploration: what scripture passage seems to fit with my idea?
- Application: what does my idea mean?

Notice, in Eisegesis, there is no examination of the words of the text or their relationship to each other, and no cross-referencing with related passages; thus, no real desire to understand the actual meaning. Scripture serves only as a prop to the interpreter's idea.

To be objective in our interpretation of Scripture is not always easy, especially when it comes to money. Money is what we all need; we cannot imagine a life without it. As a matter of fact, it would be impossible to have a normal life in this world without money.

Can you imagine how difficult it could be for a person who was raised in a church, and received all their money from the traditional tithing, and sowing and reaping teachings, to have a change of mind? We can only imagine how difficult it would be for this person who was saved, filled with the Spirit, and even attended the bible school of that church, to do a proper exegesis of a passage about money in the Bible, especially if what he has believed all his life is nowhere to be found in Scripture!

I am reminded of a time, when after I posted on Facebook about Paul falling from his horse, I was asked to point to the verse that states Paul fell from his horse. The answer was simple yet difficult to accept. There is not such a verse at all and I believed a lie for a very long time. What astounded me was the power to read something into a verse that is simply not there. Change can be difficult.

The *critical factor* in the human brain is a very powerful filter, questioning everything that contradicts what the subconscious is already persuaded of. It is what psychologists manipulate through psychotherapy and hypnosis. In psychology, we learn that the *critical factor* is a part of the conscious mind. It's like a guard at the gate between the conscious mind and the subconscious, having the power to accept or prevent suggestions from entering the subconscious mind. It has very good intentions; its job is to protect us. Because change is viewed as a threat to our nervous system, any suggestion that does not match the existing programming automatically gets rejected. That is how it accomplishes its goal of protecting us.

http://www.viahypnosis.com/whyitworks.htm

The critical factor acts as a vigilant guard against the unknown. Designed to protect you, it often rejects what is unfamiliar to it, even if it is of real benefit to you. For example, let's say your rational, conscious mind has come to realize that you have to change your belief system to change your life. Your critical factor will most likely reject this new belief system for a while, sometimes for a very long while, because it seems strange, since it has **no proof of its benefit to you**. It doesn't matter if you know consciously that the new belief will improve your life. It is unknown to the subconscious and therefore a possible threat, so the critical factor rejects it, stopping it from entering your subconscious mind.

This might sound very negative, yet there is a positive side to it. Once we do have a subconscious mind (default setting) reprogrammed by the power of the Holy Spirit, into truth, we will struggle to accept anything different than the truth we have come to believe. The critical factor is part of our God-given design to protect us. It is a beautiful, powerful protection system that will help keep you safe *once the subconscious is programmed with truth.* What I am saying is that it might be difficult for you to see truth in a Scripture when you first hear it. Since the truth you hear might even be a bit disturbing at first, what will help you to have an effective, smooth reprogramming is to know that you will be safe in the arms of your loving Father. He will do everything possible to have your heart programmed with His love and He is greater than any lie we believe!

In focusing on God's love for you, the critical factor will relax. A conducive atmosphere for reprogramming is one of love—continual, reassuring love. The more you focus on how He loves you, the easier and faster the reprogramming will be. Remember that God is greater than your subconscious mind. We also need to understand that this is not a five-minute process; it can take some time and will need confirmation, which God always provides.

Here's what this boils down to, as we connect this to money: If you have been programmed to believe the Bible states X about money, but it actually states Y, your mind will initially try to make an X out of the Y. A good example of this would be the following: If you have heard and believed that tithing to the local church is needed to assure you of blessings in the future, it will be difficult to believe you don't have to give to be protected. Even if it is proven to you from Scripture, the critical factor will not want to accept it unless the Y resembles an X. This is why people who traditionally believed in tithing, and claim to be set free, will say things like, "Under the law, we have given ten percent and now we are free from the law. We live by grace, which means we will AT LEAST give ten percent, since the standard of grace is higher than that of the law." I hope you can see how the Y is twisted into an X to compromise the truth to be acceptable for the error in the subconscious.

The critical factor will only allow teaching that confirms what it actually believes. For example, someone who claims that he does not believe in tithing but states that New Testament giving must be more than ten percent—since grace is more powerful than law—reveals what he actually believes. He believes one should tithe and all his security is built upon the traditional system that he cannot let go of. The critical factor has just taken all the good in the new revelation and twisted it to be acceptable to allow into the person's heart. This is when the conscious mind understands something to be true and life-giving, while the heart does not believe it.

To reconcile conscious truth with subconscious truth, we see the critical factor adapting the information to the original belief, or programming, in the subconscious mind. This will happen all the time since the human mind needs to find peace and live in peace with itself. It will accept both contradicting views, shaping the conscious into the image of the subconscious. This is what the Bible talks about when it mentions the double-minded man:

[7]For let not that man think that he shall receive any thing of the Lord. [8]A double minded man is unstable in all his ways (*KJV*, Jas. 1:7, 8).

A Trinity, family-orientated critical factor, which is flooded with the revelation of God's love shown in Jesus, will make all the difference in how we interpret the Bible. I won't be surprised if there has been—and will continue to be—a lot of pressure on the traditional, law-based critical factor as we look into the Scriptures that have served as the basis of our teachings on tithing, sowing and reaping. This will especially be true when I tell you that there is not a single verse in the Bible that points to tithing in the church. We can even go so far as to say that there is not a single verse in the New Testament pointing to sowing money and reaping a harvest of prosperity. "Yes, but what about this verse and that popular verse?" you might ask.

Please understand that I would not make that statement, put it in writing, and risk my neck in the church world, if I had no proof for what I say. We will carefully examine all the mainline Scriptures that are used in church and see if they actually say what we were told they say.

Jesus must have had the same problem with the critical

factor. He was born as a human being into a law-based home. He was circumcised on the 8th day, and grew up in a normal Jewish family. He knew the Scriptures and was programmed with all the traditional Jewish beliefs. I am sure He felt safe and secure in the knowledge He had of His Jewish traditions. Let's see when the Father broke through the critical factor in the mind of Jesus, revealing a powerful truth to Him, from where the life He came to give manifested. Jesus followed all the Jewish customs. So, could it be that Jesus followed the sacrificial systems of the Jews? Yes, for sure. (I am sure that some of you could already feel the critical factor rejecting what was just said. All you need to do now is to know that you are safe in the hand of God and ask Him to teach you the truth about the matter in a loving, caring atmosphere.)

The main activity of the temple was that of sacrificing. That is why there were many work groups of priests. Technically, only priests offered sacrifices, but the sacrifices were provided by worshipers, usually the male head-of- households. The worshipers brought the sacrifices (animals, wine, grain, etc.) to the prescribed place and handed them over to the priests, for the priests to perform the rituals.

The sacrificial system had been given by God. Any Jew would say that God told them to sacrifice. Jesus would have been in the same mindset, which we will look at in Scripture. The Jews offered sacrifices as peace offerings, fellowship offerings, votive offerings, and offerings of consecration. Let's consider what I am saying from the New Testament:

Luke reports that after Jesus was born, and the time of

Mary's menstrual impurity had run its course, Mary and Joseph took the baby Jesus to Jerusalem, to present Him to God at the temple. This was in keeping with Mosaic law (See Leviticus 12:6-8). We're told they offered a sacrifice in accordance with the law, a pair of two young pigeons (See Lev. 5:11).

Then there is the Last Supper, which many consider a Passover meal. John reports Jesus crucified on the day of preparation for the Passover (See John19:31). But there may have been calendrical debates going on at the time because Mark 14:12-25, along with Matthew and Luke, presents it as a Passover meal. Jesus sends two of His disciples into the city to make preparations, which likely included securing a place for the meal and securing the food itself, which would have included the lamb from the temple. Even if Jesus Himself did not sacrifice in the temple, He had others do it for Him.

By looking at all of this, we can only conclude that Jesus' mind must've been deeply programmed into the Jewish system. This was a programming that had to change. It was something placed inside the heart of Jesus by strong Jewish tradition; therefore, Jesus' Father had to bring the purpose of sacrifice to Jesus. We are going to look at how Jesus viewed the Law and all the sacrificial, ceremonial laws, and we'll see how He had a revelation of what it was actually all about. Jesus had to be reprogrammed with the true interpretation about it all:

6Sacrifice and offering thou didst not desire; mine ears hast thou opened: burnt offering and sin offering hast thou not required. 7Then said I, Lo, I come: in the volume of the book it is written of me, [8]I delight to do thy will, O my God: yea, thy law is within my heart. [9]I have preached righteousness in the great congregation: lo, I have not refrained my lips, O LORD, thou knowest (*KJV*, Ps. 40:6-9).

This is a prophetic passage that gives us perfect insight into the prayer life of Jesus. We see Jesus stating that God revealed things to Him, by opening His ears to understand what the sacrifices were really all about. He says the sacrifices were not required by God. Can you imagine what must have gone through Jesus' mind, as the inner voice of the Holy Spirit directed Him to see something that contradicted everything people believed in His day! If God opened the ears of Jesus, they must have been closed at first, right?

As the teenage Son of God walked through the temple and saw all the sacrifices, I am sure He wondered why His loving Father would allow this. His Father then revealed to Him that none of what He saw was required by God, but that the sacrifices represented the body of Jesus, which was prepared for carrying mankind's suffering of sin. Jesus went so far as to say that the Scriptures were actually speaking of Him, and not about animal sacrifice required by God. What a powerful change of mind Jesus must have had when He heard something that contradicted everything the Jews ever believed! When Jesus looked at the law, He saw it from a completely different mindset.

Just as God opened Jesus' ears, He opens ours to understand and to see even the tithe as something Jesus fulfilled. (more on this later). As we see Jesus rejoicing about God opening His ears to hear and understand the true meaning of the Scriptures, let it be an encouragement of what God will do for us as we look into the different views on tithing.

CHAPTER 10

How Jesus Read the Old Testament

In Psalm 40, it is boldly declared that the Father had no interest in sacrifice and offerings but that these things were types and shadows of what **Jesus** had to come and do, in order to bring salvation to us. So, when we read the Old Testament, we need to read it as Jesus would have read it. Jesus read it as the Father's commandment and clear-cut instruction of who He was and what He had to come and do for us. Reading the Old Testament in any other way can be very dangerous.

As we have a look at Psalm 40, we will see that it gives us insight into the prayer life of Jesus Christ. It was prophetically written in such a way that we could see what He prayed, word for word. In it we see how Jesus lived while He was on the earth, and we understand He had to live **by faith**. He did not know everything; the Holy Spirit revealed to Him who He was, and once He was persuaded of what the Holy Spirit revealed to Him, He willingly opened up His life for God to bring salvation forth through Him. The Holy Spirit started to speak to Jesus at a very young age; as a matter of fact, the Bible says, "when upon [His] mother's breasts" (*KJV*, Ps.22:9). I also believe that Mary had a lot to do with teaching Jesus about who His Father really was. The only reason I point this out is so that we can understand Psalm 40 and the context in which it is written. Let's look at Psalm 40, starting with verse 5:

5*Many, O LORD my God, are thy wonderful works which thou hast done, and thy thoughts which are to us-ward: they cannot be reckoned up in order unto thee: if I would declare and speak of them, they are more than can be numbered.* 6*Sacrifice and offering thou didst not desire; mine ears hast Thou opened: burnt offering and sin offering hast thou not required.* 7*Then said I, Lo, I come: in the volume of the book it is written of me* (*KJV*, Ps. 40:5-7).

The only way I can describe Psalm 40:5-7 is that it was the, "**Aha, now I understand!**" moment in the life of Jesus. Jesus Christ comes in Psalm 40 and bursts out with joy because He understands why all the animal sacrifices were done. When Jesus gets the revelation that animal sacrifice was just a type and shadow, and not the substance, joy bursts forth in His life. The Scripture even says, "for the joy that was set before Him, He endured the cross" (*KJV*, Heb.12:2). This is much clearer in verses 6 and 7 of Psalm 40. Let's read them again:

6*Sacrifice and offering thou didst not desire; mine ears hast Thou opened: burnt offering and sin offering hast thou not required.* 7*Then said I, Lo, I come: in the volume of the book it is written of me* (*KJV*, Ps. 40:6, 7),

Here we see Jesus realizing that God never wanted any animal sacrifice, nor did He want any offering from anybody; it was never required by the Father. What Jesus said in Psalm 40:7 is what it's all about: "In the volume of the book it is written of me." What that means is that the entire Old Covenant is all about **Jesus** and what He came to do for us.

In Hebrew, the word *volume* means *title*. The best way I can describe it is that Jesus said the law was **addressed to Him**. This can be clearly seen in Hebrews 10:

5*Wherefore when he cometh into the world, he saith, Sacrifice and offering thou wouldest not, but a body hast thou prepared me:* 6*In burnt offerings and sacrifices for sin thou hast had no pleasure.* 7*Then said I, Lo, I come (in the volume of the book it is written of me,) to do thy will, O God* (*KJV*, Heb. 10:5-7).

Here we see the writer of the book of Hebrews interprets Psalm 40 as pointing towards the **body** of Jesus Christ. He was talking about the physical body Jesus possessed, as that which the Father has prepared for the salvation of man. Therefore, it is paramount to keep in mind the Father's preparation of the physical body of Jesus Christ, for the salvation of man, when we are reading the Old Testament.

For instance, when we read about the **scapegoat** in Leviticus 16:10, we need to think of Jesus and how He would have read that message. He would ask Himself how that is related to His physical body and bringing salvation to mankind. And when we read about the **sacrificial lamb** throughout the Old Testament, we need to think of Jesus and how He understood that the lamb signifies His body. When we look at the **tithe,** we need to ask ourselves how Jesus looked at the tithe, knowing He came to fulfill all sacrifice and offerings.

The Law was Never Written to Give Us Life by Our Obedience to It

Jesus Christ came and declared the correct interpretation of the Law, which was in the context of what **He** had to do in His body to bring forth salvation to man; thus, making the Law beautiful and life-giving. If we look at the Law in any other way, it will be devastating and will destroy our lives. With all this in mind, we can understand why the Law was written. It was never written to give us life by our obedience to it; it was written **to Jesus**. To understand more of this, you can go to my website www.dynamicministries.com, and search for the message titled, *The Way Jesus Looked at the Law.*

Now let's continue in Psalm 40:

8*I delight to do thy will, O my God: yea, thy law is within*
my heart. 9*I have preached righteousness in the great congregation: lo, I have not refrained my lips, O LORD,*
thou knowest. 10*I have not hid thy righteousness within my heart; I have declared thy faithfulness and thy salvation: I have not concealed thy lovingkindness and thy truth from the great congregation* (*KJV*, Ps. 40:8-10).

Salvation is not obtained by our obedience to any type or shadow mentioned in the Old Testament.

When we look at verses 8-10, we find that Jesus Christ comes giving a **new definition** to the Law. He declares the correct interpretation of the Old Testament law as that which **He** had to do to bring forth Salvation to man.

This is the Law of God:

It is the message of how God was flooded with lovingkindness, how He has come and shown His faithfulness towards mankind, and how He showed righteousness to people in saving them from their sins. That is the law of God; that is also the law that God will write on your heart. God is not going to write the Ten Commandments or any other religious rules on your heart, for that is called the "ministration of death written on stones," according to 2 Corinthians 3:7 and other Scriptures. The only law God writes on your heart is the law that says He **saved** us by preparing a physical human body, in which the sin of the whole world could be taken away, where mankind could be represented in the Trinity and so have life!

Knowing the Bible is all about Jesus and what He came to do for mankind, how do you think Jesus read the passages about tithing? Wouldn't He see tithing as something He was to fulfill, to bring salvation to man?

CHAPTER 11

Tithing

If you have just opened to this page to read my view on tithing, I would like to advise you to read the rest of the book before reading this part. If you read this part without reading what I've said in the previous ten chapters, you might think I'm an anti-church rebel. You might even think I'm a bit crazy! And if it's you who's an anti-tithing rebel, this chapter might even be fuel for your rebellion.

It is not my intention to fuel anyone's rebellion against financial giving. I believe in generous giving. So, if you are rebelling against giving, you really need to read the first nine chapters so that you can be set free from the residue of law abuse. I am fully against anti-generous living; it is not what God intends for us nor is it the highest quality of life. I am as much against anti-giving as I am against tithing.

The Abrahamic Tithe Before the Law

We will be looking at the reason why the tithe was initiated and practiced during the time from Abraham to Moses, which of course puts it before the giving of the

Law. Once we look at the Old Testament facts, and also determine if the tithe was used by the early church, we will need to decide if this tithe system is still valid today.

It is commonly believed that Abraham tithed before the giving of the Ten Commandments. The fact that he tithed before the giving of the Law is then used as a foundation from where tithing in the New Testament is preached. The basic reasoning is that everything prior to the giving of the Law is not subject to the fulfillment of the law, making tithing a valid New Testament principle because it occurred before the Law was given in written format.

This very popular argument, in defence of the tithe, goes like this: *Oh sure, we hear you saying that we are putting people under the law to expect them to tithe, but what about Abraham? He tithed BEFORE the law, did he not?*

Let's have a look at this reasoning to see if it can stand in the presence of the finished work of Jesus and the love God has for us. First, we need to set the hermeneutical parameters so that we can look at the life of Abraham and tithing. We always need to look at Scripture in line with the following:

- *The World Behind the Text* - this is author- centered, and it is a description of the thought world and the setting of the life of the text. It also presents a rationale for historical research, and highlights the need for study of biblical languages.

- *The World Within the Text* - this is the text as a literary unit, which details examples of genre and subgenre within literature, generally, then analyses of both the Old and New Testaments, in the light of their literary characteristics, enlivening the discussion with frequent examples.

- *The World in Front of the Text* - this is what the text communicates to the reader who understands the world behind and the world inside the text.

- *The Character of God* - as seen in Jesus, the perfect interpretation of Scripture.

- *The Fulfillment in Jesus* - this is how the text points to what is demonstrated in Jesus and what He accomplished in all He did in the incarnation, death and resurrection.

- *Harmony* - with the rest of Scripture.

(Although what I wrote in my study is along the lines of the hermeneutical outline given above, it is not documented in that order—although all the principles were followed. If we were to answer every teaching in the order above, this book would be a 700-page book that would not reach the goal for which it is written.)

Interpretation of Scripture must be in agreement with the rest of the Bible, or we can easily end up with an eisegesis instead of a healthy exegesis. If we reason that Abraham tithed before the Law, thus making it part of what we need to do in the New Testament, we will have to conclude that everything Abraham did before the Law is something that should be done in the church today. We will then have to apply that hermeneutical principle to all elements of what Abraham did before the Law, to make our interpretation healthy. Should we not do it, we will be walking on the slippery slope of eisegetical interpretation of Scripture. The principle should be absolute and true for all things that happened before the giving of the Law or it cannot be true for anything. The statement that we need to tithe, because Abraham tithed before the Law, is a perfect example of an eisegetical take on a passage. We will see this clearly as we continue to study the concept in question.

Let's have a look at things Abraham did prior to the giving of the Law and see if it can fit the New Testament parameters and what Jesus clearly portrayed in the incarnation, death and resurrection:

- Abraham was circumcised before the Law.
- Marriage to close family members was allowed, for Abraham was married to his own half-sister:
    - *Besides, she actually is my sister, the daughter of my father, but not the daughter of my mother, and she became my wife* (*NKJV*, Gen 20:12).
- Animal sacrifice was clearly demanded by God before the Law:
    - *9So He said to him, "Bring Me a three year old heifer, and a three year old female goat, and a three year old ram, and a turtledove, and a young pigeon." 10Then he brought all these to Him and cut them in two, and laid each half opposite the other; but he did not cut the birds* (*NASB*, Gen. 15:9, 10).

Let us ask the following questions:

- Is **animal sacrifice** part of the New Testament Church?
- Do we see **marriage to family members** encouraged in the New Testament?
- Is **circumcision** a New Testament principle?

Obviously, the answer to all of the above questions is no. If we follow healthy hermeneutical guidelines, we can conclude that it would not be possible for tithing to be in the New Testament on the basis that people tithed before the Law. Tithing seen in the Old Testament does not prove it can be in the New Testament. If it did, practicing every pre-law principle, such as marriage to family members, circumcision, and sacrifice of animals would also apply.

The truth is, we cannot state that anything prior to the giving of the Ten Commandments is to be done in the New Testament! Should we do that, it would not be congruent with the incarnation, the cross, or what was accomplished in the resurrection. We can clearly see that although animal sacrifice and circumcision were practiced by Abraham long before the Law, it is not acceptable in the New Testament. The following story illustrates how ridiculous that would be:

A church member announces, "I am going to marry my sister and slaughter a bull for a sacrifice to God."

The church leader gasps, "Are you crazy?! Why would you want to do that?"

"I have discovered a powerful truth in the Scriptures! Abraham married his own sister and sacrificed BEFORE the Law was given," the church member explains, "Since Abraham did that before the law, I have the right to do it today. I have always loved my sister; hallelujah!!"

Frowning, the church leader continues, "Something is very wrong here. You know better than that, don't you? You are completely wrong in the way you look at what happened before the Law. It would be a sin to do what you want to do, so just know that you cannot get married in our church. You also need to consider that you will be locked up for sacrificing an animal. What is wrong with you?!"

The church member tries to defend his reasoning, "Well, Abraham tithed before the Law and that is why I tithe. Tithing before the Law is a grace principle, is it not?"

The church leader doesn't want to discuss it anymore, "Let me think about it." Then, to his wife that evening he groans, "We have a church member that has lost his mind and is becoming extremely difficult."

Abraham Tithed to Earthly Kings

The Abrahamic tithe, in its true context, is something that we have not really been introduced to in the modern-day church. Abraham's background, and the culture in which he lived, was radically different than what we are used to in the western world. Since Abraham lived in a day and age when the land was filled with kings and their kingdoms, we need to study this out, in order to understand why he would do such a thing as tithe to a king. Only when we understand this, will we know what a wonderful connection it has to the here and now. Let's have a look at the New Testament connection most people make between Abraham and tithing.

The only sound New Testament application of tithing, and the message it was intended to convey, can be found in Hebrews 7:1-28. But Hebrews 7 is one of the most difficult chapters to explain to people who lack understanding of ancient Babylonian-Chaldean, cultural practices. As a matter of fact, it would be impossible to explain without having knowledge of the ancient practices. We are going to have a proper look at the ancient practices and see what we can conclude from it in regard to tithing, discussed in Hebrews.

Before we go any farther, let's have a look at what Hebrews 7 actually communicates. Hebrews 7 explains the passing away of the Law and the authority Jesus had to end it. The passage explains that Jesus was of higher priestly order than Levi, and even higher than Abraham. Since Jesus was of higher rank than the Levitical order, the law of Levi had to submit to the law of Jesus (called the *law of life*). Jesus had authority to bring in a new law and end the old; that is all the passage teaches. When Abraham tithed to Melchizedek, it meant that Abraham saw himself as lesser and submitted to Melchizedek (let's call him Mel). Since the Levites received tithes in the Levitical order, it was recognized that they had a very high order, for under it the LAW was given. The Hebrews writer then explains that Levi is of lower order than Abraham, since Abraham was the father of Levi, making Levi lower than Mel. Should there be a priest in the order of Mel he would have power over the Levitical order and therefore be able to change the law, given in the power of the Levitical priesthood. (The Levitical priesthood was in the order of

Aaron, which was a lower order than that of Melchizedek.) The Hebrews writer then explains how Jesus came in the order of Melchizedek, ended the Law of Moses, and brought a new law.

The error being taught is the following:

When we tithe to the local church, we are paying tithes in Abraham to Melchizedek, which is Jesus. And if we do that, we give tithes to Jesus. Oh my goodness… there could not be a better example of eisegesis than this interpretation! It is absolutely out of context and has no scriptural backing. It is just reading into the verse what is believed and nothing healthy is extracted from the verse.

Abram's Move from Babylonian-ruled Mesopotamia

Abram was not a Christian and did not grow up in the Bible Belt. We need to know that Abram was under an AMORITE, who enforced the Babylonian-Chaldean law on all who lived in his fields. As a child, Abram—who would eventually be called *Abraham*—lived in Ur, then moved to Haran after some years. It was at Haran that God told him to leave everything and go to a land God would show him (See Gen. 12). He eventually ended up close to Hebron, in the fields of Mamre, an **Amorite**, south of Salem (Jerusalem). It is very important for us to understand that Abraham was living and following a Babylonian-Chaldean tax system of honoring the greater, called *the tithe tax*.

The King's Tithe

What is the kingly tithe? The king's tithe was a

Babylonian tax system whereby you honored the king and his rule over you. All the subjects of the king had to give ten percent of their income to the king. That is how they showed their respect to the king and submitted to him. Should you not pay it you would be under the curse of the king, seen as his enemy and punished.

The closest we have to the king's tithe in our day is taxation. Taxation is the closest, but not exactly what took place between Abraham and Melchizedek in Genesis 14. It was something that was not given voluntarily, but by compulsion, to pay respect to the king. If anyone did not tithe to the king, they would come under his curse, which meant jail or even death.

There are three places in the Bible that definitely talk about the **king's tithe**:

Genesis 14:17-20
1 Samuel 8:4-22
Hebrews 7:1-20

Let's first look at the king's tithe in **1 Samuel 8**, so that we can understand the reasoning in Hebrews 7 and Genesis 14:

4 Then all the elders of Israel gathered themselves together, and came to Samuel unto Ramah, 5 And said unto him, Behold, thou art old, and thy sons walk not in thy ways: now make us a king to judge us like all the nations.
6 But the thing displeased Samuel, when they said, give us a king to judge us. And Samuel prayed unto the LORD.
7 And the LORD said unto Samuel, hearken unto the voice of the people in all that they say unto thee: for they

have not rejected thee, but they have rejected me, that I should not reign over them. 8According to all the works which they have done since the day that I brought them up out of Egypt even unto this day, wherewith they have forsaken me, and served other gods, so do they also unto thee. 9Now therefore hearken unto their voice: howbeit yet protest solemnly unto them, and show them the manner of the king that will reign over them.10And Samuel told all the words of the LORD unto the people that asked of him a king. 11And he said, This will be the manner of the king that will reign over you: He will take your sons, and appoint them for himself, for his chariots, and to be his horsemen; and some will run before his chariots. 12And he will appoint him captains over thousands, and captains over fifties; and will set them to ear his ground, and to reap his harvest, and to make his instruments of war, and instruments of his chariots. 13And he will take your daughters to be confectionaries, and to be cooks, and to be bakers. 14And he will take your fields, and your vineyards, and your olive yards, even the best of them, and give them333 to his servants. ***15And he will take the tenth of your seed,*** *and of your vineyards, and give to his officers, and to his servants. 16And he will take your menservants, and your maidservants, and your goodliest young men, and your asses, and put them to his work.* ***17He will take the tenth of your sheep****: and ye will be his servants 18And ye shall cry out in that day because of your king which ye shall have chosen you; and the Lord will not hear you in that day. 19Nevertheless the people refused to obey the voice of Samuel; and they said, Nay; but we will have a king over us; 20That we also may be* *like all the nations; and that our king may judge us, and go out before us, and fight our battles. [21]And Samuel heard all the words of the people, and he rehearsed them in the ears of the Lord. [22]And the Lord said to Samuel, hearken unto their voice, and make them a king. And Samuel said unto the men of Israel, Go ye every man unto his city* (*KJV*, 1 Sam. 8:4-22).

This is the record of the hardened Israelites rejecting God as their king, while instead wanting Samuel to give them a king, "**like all the nations**." So God gave them a king just like all the other nations, as they had requested, and He said the king would be as the other pagan and Babylonian kings. When we look at the kingly system, we find that some of the tithes they had to give were tithes of sheep and grain. In the case of Abraham, we find that tithes were even given of the spoils of war.

It would be a good thing to find other writing outside of the Bible to see what these Babylonian kings and their codes of law were all about. Thanks be to God that there are other writings that are well preserved, even better preserved than the original documents of the Bible. I will be explaining these historical systems so that we can better understand the death Israel was giving into.

In the following passages we will be comparing what the Israelites were promised, and the one-tenth tax system they were giving themselves into, when they asked for a king. The system they wanted was common; it was in practice even before the birth of Abram:

And he will take the tenth of your seed, and of your vineyards, and give to his officers and to his servants

(*KJV*, 1Sam. 8:15).

"He will take the tenth of your sheep: and ye will be his servants" (*KJV*, 1Sam. 8:17).

The *masretu* —the Ugarit and Babylonian one-tenth tax

Tithing to a local king was the custom of the day. Abraham did not tithe because God was writing a spiritual, eternal 10% law on his heart. The tithing law was a Babylonian Ugarit practice of acknowledging kingship over you. It was a taxation system of the unbelievers and sinners.

Hebrew is a Semitic language, related to Akkadian, the language that was widely used as a means of communication among speakers of other languages of that time. Listed below are some specific instances of the Mesopotamian tithe, taken from *The Assyrian Dictionary of the Oriental Institute of the University of Chicago, Vol. 4 "E"[3]*

Referring to a ten percent tax levied on garments by the local ruler: "the palace has taken eight garments as your tithe (on 85 garments)"

"... eleven garments as tithe (on 112 garments)" "... (the sun-god) Shamash demands the tithe ..."

"...four minas of silver, the tithe of [the gods] Bel, Nabu, and Nergal ..."

"... he has paid, in addition to the tithe for Ninurta, the

tax of the gardiner"

"... the tithe of the chief accountant, he has delivered it to [the sun-god] Shamash"

"... why do you not pay the tithe to the Lady-of-Uruk?"

"... (a man) owes barley and dates as balance of the tithe of the years three and four"

"... the tithe of the king on barley of the town ..."

"... with regard to the elders of the city whom (the king) has summoned to (pay) tithe ..."

"... the collector of the tithe of the country Sumundar ..."

"... (the official Ebabbar in Sippar) who is in charge of the tithe ..."

History reveals that tithing existed in ancient Babylon, Persia, Egypt, and China - but only for political or societal purposes, **not for giving to God in order to be blessed**. It was a taxation system paid to the ruler or king over the people.

Abraham must've been well-acquainted with the Babylonian tithing system when he moved from Ur. Ur was a Babylonian city in the land of the Chaldeans, which was known for the idols they made and sold. Abraham had to be very familiar with the religious customs of giving tithes to the kings. He was raised in a region where tithing was practiced as a custom in honoring one's king.

Abram and the Sky God

And there came one that had escaped, and told Abram the Hebrew; for he dwelt in the plain of Mamre the Amorite, brother of Eshcol, and brother of Aner: and these were confederate with Abram (*KJV*, Gen. 14:13).

Abraham lived in the fields of Mamre, and so did his brothers, who are identified by some commentaries as *chiefs* or *kings*. I am willing to make the assumption that Abram paid tithes to Mamre, or to his superior, since he lived in his fields. If Abram had his own army and the ability to overthrow other kings, Mamre and his brothers would be crazy not to ask for Abram's ten-percent, to make sure that he honored them as landowners, and chiefs or kings. It was common practice for countries to ask for taxes from their immigrants, for if an immigrant could not benefit the king, why would he want him there? This is not eisegesis, I am not putting something into the text but drawing from the world before and the world within the text, as the parameters for our hermeneutical study.

The full Hebrew name for the fields of Mamre where Abram lived is *Elonei Mamre*, which refers to a cultic shrine dedicated to the supreme sky god, "El," of the Canaanites, whom they referred to as "god." It was a place where there were trees that the people believed had special powers to help them connect with "god." Abram decided to build an altar at that place, sacrificing to the god he believed told him to move to another place. Here we see Abraham still mixing his beliefs with the beliefs and practices of that day. Abraham went to the magic trees in hopes that they could help him connect with God.

We need to realize that Abram was not a Christian at all, and he submitted to the heathen laws of those times. He lived by the rules and laws that governed the people of that time, which were what the Israelites later wanted when they asked for a king **as the other nations had**. These rules and laws applied to slavery and tithing, as we can see in the Mesopotamian tithing laws, and in 1 Sam 8:15-17 where they asked for a king.

We even see Abram and Sarah following the laws of that time in marriage. The Nuzi Tablets, as well as the old Assyrian marriage contracts, allowed for a woman to give her maidservant to her husband, to bear children for her. This was to prevent the husband from divorcing his wife if they had been childless for 10 years. When Sarah gave Hagar to Abram, they were following this common practice of their time. The laws of the land also included the one- tenth tax law, which was active in the land of the Amorites as well as Babylon.

By looking at this, we can clearly see that tithing was **not** Abraham's obedience to God. It was not some new rule that Abraham came up with, nor was it something demanded by God, but simply a widely practiced custom that people followed at the time. We know that it was a custom in the Salem area, when Melchizedek received tithes from Abram.

Abraham and Sarah Under a Law That is Not Needed Today

Although, under Babylonian law, monogamy was the rule, in the case of a childless wife, she was permitted to give her husband a maidservant to bear him children, who were then reckoned to be hers. The code did not allow the husband to take a concubine; but if his wife did not bear him a child he could do so. The concubine was a co-wife, though not of the same rank; the first wife had no power over her. Sara was observing this law when she gave Hagar to her husband Abraham for a wife, to bear children to them.

Sara was obviously observing the Code of Hammurabi when she gave Hagar to Abraham. Should we also allow this today, since it was before the Ten Commandments? Never! And we don't tithe just because tithing was practiced back then either. Tithing is much more beautiful than giving ten percent to the church. You will understand what I mean as I continue to explain what tithing really is. It would be completely wrong to think Abraham tithed under grace, making it the foundation from where we tithe in the church today. It would simply be an assumption that has absolutely no reference at all. We can even go so far as to say it is deception.

Abram Meets Melchizedek

So, what really happened when Abram tithed to Melchizedek? When Melchizedek, who was King of Salem, brought Abram bread and wine, and blessed him, Abram gave him a tenth of the spoils taken from battle, as it is written in Genesis 14:

18 And Melchizedek king of Salem brought out bread and wine: and he was priest of the highest God. 19 And he blessed him, and said, Blessed be Abram of the highest God, possessor of heaven and earth: 20 And blessed be the highest God, which hath delivered thine enemies into thy hand. And he gave him tithes of all (*KJV*, Gen. 14:18-20).

Tithes were only given to people who were of higher rank.

It was the honor shown to the higher ranking person, as the king or superior, acknowledging that the person was greater than the one giving the tithes. The one giving the tithe was demonstrating that the receiver of the tithe was greater as his superior.

It is also very important to understand that, while the lesser tithed to the greater, he could not *bless* the greater. For example, I could not go to a king and bless him by saying, "Blessed are you, oh king." That was not acceptable and was seen as an attack on the king. **In ancient tradition, the greater always blessed the lesser. This is a very important point to remember, since this is the foundation for the writer's reasoning in Hebrews, when he talks about the ending of the law and the order of Melchizedek.**

The King of Sodom

8 *And there went out the king of Sodom, and the king of*
Gomorrah, and the king of Admah, and the king of
Zeboiim, and the king of Bela (the same is Zoar;) and they
joined battle with them in the vale of Siddim; 9 *With*
Chedorlaomer the king of Elam, and with Tidal king of
nations, and Amraphel king of Shinar, and Arioch king of
Ellasar; four kings with five. 10 *And the vale of Siddim was*
full of slime pits; and the kings of Sodom and Gomorrah
fled, and fell there; and they that remained fled to the
mountain. 11 *And they took all the goods of Sodom and*
Gomorrah, and all their victuals, and went their way.
12 *And they took Lot, Abram's brother's son, who dwelt in*
Sodom, and his goods, and departed. 13 *And there came*

*one that had escaped, and told Abram the Hebrew; for he
dwelt in the plain of Mamre the Amorite, brother of
Eshcol, and brother of Aner: and these were confederate
with Abram.* 14*And when Abram heard that his brother
was taken captive, he armed his trained servants, born in
his own house, three hundred and eighteen, and pursued
them unto Dan.* 15*And he divided himself against hem, he
and his servants, by night, and smote them, and pursued
them unto Hobah, which is on the left hand of Damascus.*
16 *And he brought back all the goods, and also brought
again his brother Lot, and his goods, and the women also,
and the people.* 17*And the king of Sodom went out to meet
him after his return from the slaughter of Chedorlaomer,
and of the kings that were with him, at the valley of
Shaveh, which is the king's dale.* 18*And Melchizedek king
of Salem brought forth bread and wine: and he was the
priest of the most high God.* 19*And he blessed him, and
said, Blessed be Abram of the most high God, possessor
of heaven and earth:* 20*And blessed be the most high God,
which hath delivered thine enemies into thy hand. And he
gave him tithes of all.* 21*And the king of Sodom said unto
Abram, Give me the persons, and take the goods to
thyself.* 22*And Abram said to the king of Sodom, I have
lift up mine hand unto the LORD, the most high God, the
possessor of heaven and earth,* 23*That I will not take from
a thread even to a shoelatchet, and that I will not take
anything that is thine, lest thou shouldest say, I have made
Abram rich:* 24*Save only that which the young men have
eaten, and the portion of the men which went with me,
Aner, Eshcol, and Mamre; let them take their portion*
(*KJV*, Gen. 14:8-24).

This passage basically explains that Abram made war against Chedorlaomer, a king that overpowered the King of Sodom, where Abram's nephew Lot lived. When Lot was taken hostage, Abram did not like that at all, so he went after Chedorlaomer and conquered him. On his return, Abram entered the king's valley, outside of Salem, and passed through the land ruled by King Melchizedek. This is when **Melchizedek blessed Abram**, and gave him bread and wine. In return, **Abram gave Melchizedek tithes of all the spoils.**

Understanding what actually happened here is of utmost importance. The fact that Abram made use of the tithe in his dealings with Melchizedek is amazing, because Abram was not under the jurisdiction of Melchizedek. Since Abram lived in the field of Mamre, the king over Mamre should have received his tithe. Abraham was so amazed by this man called *Melchizedek*—the king of Salem and the priest of the highest god El-yone—that he decided to declare *him* as his king, instead of honoring and tithing to the king of his jurisdiction. Melchizedek was different than any other king, because he was not only a king but also a priest—and that of the "highest god."

As Abram continued on his journey, he met up with the King of Sodom, probably at the place where Abram stayed in the fields of Mamre. Even though Abram was victorious in battle against Chedorlaomer and gained all the spoils that previously belonged to the King of Sodom, he refused to take any of those spoils that Chedorlaomer had obtained in his victory over the King of Sodom; he refused because he had lifted his hand in oath to the highest God. How did he do that? He acknowledged God as king in giving His Priest, Melchizedek (the one that represented Him), a tithe according to the Amorite-Babylonian tithe system. When Abram gave the tithe to Melchizedek, he was making Melchizedek his king, and in doing that he declared him as his superior. Since Melchizedek was the king **and** priest of the highest God, he represented the highest God on Earth, thus Abram made the highest God his King in what he did according to his custom.

The fact that tithing was seen as acknowledgement of kingship is the foundation for Hebrews 7. The lesser always tithed to the greater and the lesser is always blessed by the greater. By seeing this truth, we will also understand how the Abrahamic tithe is fulfilled in *our* lives. To try to make giving ten percent to the local church a foundation for honoring Jesus would be a perfect example of an eisegesis. If you have read this into Scripture, and your heart is drawn to this eisegesis, it could be that the god of this world has blinded your mind and heart. Why would you want to see something in the Scriptures that is just not there? God can and will free you from confusion, as He has helped me. It took Him a while to get me to understand the Order of Melchizedek and I trust that I will be able to explain it in a very easy to understand manner.

Clear Understanding

It is difficult to explain the Order of Melchizedek because we have been so indoctrinated with legalism in the area of tithing. And without understanding the word "order," we will never understand Hebrews 7, so let's look at these verses first:

"Called of God an high priest after the **order** of Melchizedek" (*KJV*, Heb. 5:10).

"Of whom we have many things to say, and hard to be uttered, seeing ye are **dull of hearing**" (*KJV*, Heb. 5:11).

The word *order* means *pattern or methodical arrangement of things*. There were basically two orders of priesthood that were of importance in the Bible: the Order of Aaron and the Order of Melchizedek. To qualify to be a priest according to the Order of Aaron, you had to fulfill certain criteria. To be a priest according to the order, or basic pattern found in Melchizedek, you also had to meet certain criteria. Please note that the context of Hebrews 7 is order of priesthood and nothing else.

The priestly Order of Aaron demanded the following criteria:

- Must be of the priestly lineage of Levi
- Must be thirty years of age

The criteria for being a priest according to the Order of Melchizedek were as follows:

- Must have no priestly genealogy
- Must be a priest and a king
- Must possess eternal life

What this means is that no Levite could ever fulfill the Order of Melchizedek; only a person who had conquered death and possessed immortality could be that priest.

It is of utmost importance to understand ranking, according

to the old Hebrew system. Abraham was honored as the highest person in Jewish history, because he was the one to whom the promise was given. Also, a father was always higher in rank than his children and naturally had authority over them. It was the fathers who blessed the children, for they were greater than their children and much greater than their grandchildren.

Abraham had Isaac, Isaac had Jacob, and Jacob had Levi. The descendants of Levi were called the Levites. The Levites did the Levitical priestly duties, under the Order of Aaron, by which they also received the law. Abraham had authority over Isaac, Isaac was greater than Jacob and Jacob than Levi. And Levi had power to receive tithes from the people, making Abraham the greatest of all, except for the one he saw as greater than himself, which was Melchizedek. Abraham demonstrated that he considered Melchizedek to be greater than himself, by tithing to him according the worldly system of that time.

Ranking order

Melchizedek

Abraham

Isaac

Jacob

Levi

Jewish Nations

Please hear me when I say this: the priesthood and kingship of Melchizedek was the **greatest of all**. If Melchizedek had walked into the land where Isaac lived, Melchizedek would have ruled over Isaac to change things in that area as he liked. The same would be true if Melchizedek were to meet with Levi. Levi would immediately submit to the law of Melchizedek, in lieu of his own laws.

With all this said, we come to the same conclusion as the writer of Hebrews: the order of Melchizedek is higher than that of Aaron (which was the Levitical priesthood), and even higher than Abraham himself, since under the Babylonian law, the lesser Abraham tithed to the greater Melchizedek. The writer of Hebrews also concludes that the Levitical laws, and way of governing, would have to give in and be declared as null and void, if a priest or king were to arise after the Order of Melchizedek, since it is an order of higher power. The Hebrews writer even concludes that there should, by necessity, be a change of law when a priest of higher order arises. This would be highly unlikely to the Jews since this priest would have to possess immortality.

But God declared that there would arise such a priest and he would fulfill the Levitical law, rendering it over and done with. The priest would then change the law to the law by which he would rule. Here is the Scripture proving it:

4*The LORD hath sworn, and will not repent, Thou art a*
priest for ever after the order of Melchizedek. 5*The Lord*
at thy right hand will strike through kings in the day of his
wrath. 6*He will judge among the heathen, he will fill the*
places with the dead bodies; he will wound the heads over
many countries. 7*He will drink of the brook in the way:*
therefore, will he lift up the head (*KJV*, Psalm 110:4-7).

"Was Melchizedek the Pre-incarnate Christ?"

It is also taught that Melchizedek was the pre-incarnate Christ receiving tithes. This logic is then used as the foundation from where we, in the Church, should tithe, validating tithing in the New Testament. Let us test this logic and see if it is true:

If this popular assertion was true, that Melchizedek was actually Jesus Himself and that He received tithes, then Jesus would have been receiving tithes from His disciples, wouldn't He? I cannot imagine Jesus telling His disciples, "You owe Me ten percent of your money because it's what belongs to Me." Or, maybe He'd say, "If you don't give Me ten percent, you are not acknowledging Me as your king." It has not been recorded in any of the Gospels that Jesus ever received a tithe.

While there have been many debates about this, I want to settle it once and for all. Only if we misunderstand the context and purpose of Hebrews 7 will we conclude that Jesus was Melchizedek. The Bible only says that Christ is a priest "**after the order of**" or "**according to**" the Order of Melchizedek—not that Jesus WAS Melchizedek (See Heb. 5:6,10; 6:20; 7:11)

The phrase "according to," in the Greek, means *in accordance with, corresponding to.* Hence, a comparison is being drawn. What this means is that the text does not say Jesus was Melchizedek, but that the order of priesthood Jesus had could be compared with, or likened to, that of Melchizedek. Since Jesus is in the same order, He was the fulfillment of Psalm 110, wherein God states that He would raise up a priest according to the order of

Melchizedek.

The order Melchizedek was in, "without father, without mother" (Heb. 7:3), implies the following: Melchizedek did not have his divine role genealogically. In like manner, Jesus' priesthood was not determined by physical lineage, as the Aaronic priesthood was, for He was of the tribe of Judah. (See Exod. 28:1; Num. 3:10).

Among the Tel el Armarna tablets, discovered in Egypt in 1887, are many letters written to a Pharaoh, from one who is called "King of Uru-Salim." The Canaanite king of "Uru-Salem" (which could be Jerusalem today), tells the Egyptian ruler that he did not receive his reign from his father and mother, but it had been conferred upon him by "the Mighty King" (See A.H. Sayce, *Melchizedek*, Dictionary of the Bible, James Hastings, Ed., Edinburgh: T.&T. Clark, 1908, III, p. 335).[

Melchizedek's administration as a normal man and not the incarnate Christ, was without "beginning of day," and "end of life." The meaning of this statement, in Hebrews 7:3, is that his priesthood was not for a fixed term, as in the case of the Levitical priests. In the Old Testament, priests began their service as priests at the age of 30 and were allowed to serve until the age of 50 (See Num. 4:3; 8:24-25).

When we look at the Melchizedek priesthood, we find absolutely no chronological limitation, with reference to his priesthood, as the "priest of the Most High God." This is a perfect **foreshadowing of Jesus**, who serves continually as our priest, since He was raised from the dead to be a priest forever.

That Melchizedek was not the same person as Jesus is clear, for Scripture declares him to only be "**like unto**" the Son of God, clearly pointing to a copy of and likening one to the other.

Without father, without mother, without descent, having neither beginning of days, nor end of life; but made like unto the Son of God; abideth a priest continually (*KJV*, Heb. 7:3).

"**Like unto**" *G871 aphomoioo*

Thayer Greek Definition:

- *to cause a model to pass off into an image or shape like it*
- *to express itself in it, to copy*
- *to produce a facsimile*
- *to be made like, render similar*

Part of Speech: verb
A Related Word by Thayer's/Strong's Number: from G575 and G3666
Citing in TDNT: 5:198, 684 [6]

The point is repeated in verse 15 of Hebrews 7: Jesus is a priest after the "**likeness**" of Melchizedek.

"The [Greek] verb *aphomoioo* always assumes two distinct and separate identities, one of which is a copy of the other. Thus Melchizedek and the Son of God are represented as two separate persons, the first of which resembles the second" (*Melchizedek*, The International Standard Bible Encyclopaedia –Revised, G.W. Bromiley,

Ed., Grand Rapids: Eerdmans, 1986, Vol. 3, p. 313). [7]

The clearest distinction between Christ and Melchizedek is found in Psalm 110:4. In this text, when David talks about what the Lord God has sworn, he quotes God, who addresses David's "Lord" (Jesus) in the second person, then refers to Melchizedek in the third person:

The Lord has sworn. And will not relent, "You, [David's Lord Jesus], are a priest forever according to the order of Melchizedek" (Ps. 110:4).

So you see, we cannot say the ancient Melchizedek was Jesus, but we can say the order of their priesthoods was the same. With all this information at hand, we can have a fresh look at what happened when Abraham tithed to Melchizedek and its relevance for the early church, the letter to the Hebrews, and for us.

Conclusion

In conclusion, we are going to go through Hebrews 7, verse by verse, explaining it in its original context. I would like you to read Hebrews 7:1-17, with all the information I have shared about Abraham, Melchizedek, Mamre, and the King of Sodom in mind:

For this Melchizedek, king of Salem and priest of the Most High God, met Abraham returning from the slaughter of the kings and blessed him (*MKJV*, Heb. 7:1).

To him Abraham also gave a tenth of all. He was first by interpretation king of righteousness, and after that also king of Salem, which is king of peace (*MKJV*, Heb. 7:2),

In these two verses, the Hebrew writer gives evidence that Melchizedek is higher than Abraham, based on the tithing and blessing principles of that time. The lesser always gave to the greater and the greater blessed the lesser.

...without father, without mother, without descent, having neither beginning of days nor end of life, but made like the Son of God, he remains a priest continually (*MKJV*, Heb. 7:3).

Paul argues that the higher order priesthood of Melchizedek has never stopped, since there is no record of the genealogy to prove the end of the Melchizedek priesthood.

Now consider how great this man was, to whom even the patriarch Abraham gave the tenth of the spoils (*MKJV*, Heb. 7:4).

The Hebrew writer points, specifically, to the greatness of Melchizedek, even greater than Abraham.

And truly they who are of the sons of Levi, who receive the office of the priest, have a commandment to take tithes of the people according to the Law, that is, from their brothers, though they come out of the loins of Abraham .[6]*But he whose descent is not counted from them received tithes from Abraham and blessed him who had the promises.*[7]*And without all contradiction the lesser is blessed by the better.*[8]*And here men who die receive tithes; but there he receives them, of whom it is witnessed that he lives* (*MKJV*, Heb. 7:6-8).

"And here men who die receive tithes" - under the Levitical priesthood, the Levites who died received tithes. Please note that it does not refer to the church meetings at all, nor to pastors who die. To say that the verse refers to dying pastors that receive tithes is the worst interpretation of the passage imaginable; it would be eisegesis in its purist form. This is done to validate tithing in the church. We cannot use this passage, in context, to prove the early church received tithes. That is eisegetical and simply a lie born from an unrenewed belief system of fear.

Please note that this "witness that he lives" refers to the record of no genealogy, NOT the tithing. The tithing is the witness of the greatness of Mel's priesthood. The lack of a priestly register points to the eternal priesthood.

Let us look at verse 8 again and I will add context comments into the passage:

8 And here [under the Levitical priesthood], men who die receive tithes [men who are not in the order of Melchizedek, since they are not possessing immortality, disqualifying the Levitical priesthood to be the fulfilment of Ps 110]; but there [when Abraham gave] he receives them, of whom it is witnessed that he lives [since there is no record of his genealogy] (*MKJV*, Heb. 7:6-8).

I would like to repeat myself.

"And **here** men that die receive tithes" - under the Levitical priesthood, the Levites that died received tithes. Please note that it does not refer to the church meetings at all, nor to pastors that die. To say that the verse refers to dying pastors that receive tithes is the worst interpretation of the passage imaginable. It would be eisegesis in its purist form. This is what is done to validate tithing in the church. We cannot use this passage in context to prove the early church received tithes. That is eisegetical and simply a lie, born from a fear-driven belief system of bondage.

That would be injecting your belief into the text. It would be another wonderful example of the critical factor in the brain twisting and reshaping of a Y to look like the acceptable X. It is just a declaration that the subconscious still believes in the tithing law. It is simply not written there or anywhere; a statement like that would be what we call an eisegesis.

9And if I may say so, Levi, also, who receives tithes, paid tithes in Abraham. 10For he was still in the loins of his father when Melchizedek met him (*MKJV*, Heb. 7:9, 10).

The writer emphasizes that a person who was not a Levite—in this case Melchizedek—received tithes from Abraham, bringing attention to a non-Levitical, everlasting priesthood greater than that of Levi.

11Therefore if perfection were by the Levitical priesthood [for under it the people received the Law], what further need was there that another priest should rise after the order of Melchizedek, and not be called after the order of Aaron? (*MKJV*, Heb. 7:11).

The writer refers to Psalm 110, when he says that another priest will arise under a different priesthood. This would be on account of the weakness of the first to make things perfect, making it an imperfect priesthood.

*12For the priesthood being changed, there is of necessity a
change made in the law also. 13For He of whom these
things are spoken belongs to another tribe, from which no
man gave attendance at the altar. 14For it is evident that
our Lord sprang out of Judah, of which tribe Moses spoke
nothing concerning priesthood* (*MKJV*, Heb. 7:12-14).

Here Paul is carefully drawing the comparison between the order of Melchizedek and that in which Jesus stands.

*15And it is still far more evident, since there arises another
priest after the likeness of Melchizedek, 16who is made,
not according to the law of a fleshly commandment, but
according to the power of an endless life. 17For He
testifies, "You are a priest forever after the order of
Melchizedek." 18For truly there is a putting away of the
commandment which went before, because of the
weakness and unprofitableness of it. 19For the Law made
nothing perfect, but the bringing in of a better hope did,
by which we draw near to God* (*MKJV*, Heb. 7:15-19).

Paul declares Jesus as the perfect match for the Order of Melchizedek, therefore announcing the end of the Levitical law, and introducing faith unto righteousness because of the fulfilled law. Paul is talking about the change of law in Hebrews 7, which would be total, absolute madness to a Jew. Any religious Jew, then or nowadays, could not even begin to fathom that the law would ever be done away with. Paul tries to explain there is room for a change and the ending of the law, using the argument of higher order having power over lower order to prove his case.

I hope you can see how wrong it would be to try and use this passage to institute tithing in church; it would be an absolute abuse of the passage. We are not under the Babylonian custom anymore, nor is it used as a system to provide for the church in the book of Acts or anywhere else. If we are going to look at Israel as our example, then tithing (giving ten percent of your money) is what we will have to do, but only when we have a king we are not supposed to have.

There is a way we participate in the tithe of Abraham: we simply believe in Jesus, confessing Him as Lord. If you would like to live in a place where you mix ancient Babylonian tradition with Christianity, in tithing to acknowledge kingship, it will only be based on personal preference and not biblical command or suggestion.

CHAPTER 12

Jesus as the Tithe

In this chapter, we are going to look at what tithing under the Levitical priesthood foreshadowed. We need to understand that reading and comprehending Scripture cannot be separated from the Divine Ones and the dynamics in the Trinity. Let's enter into the Trinity and see the dynamics of Father, Son and Holy Spirit at work in our approach to Scripture. This is exciting and life giving! Here we go!

I am going to explain to you that **JESUS is the tithe**, that the manna in the Ark of the Covenant pointed to Jesus, and that the tithe in the storehouse is the body of Jesus broken for us. The Scripture we are about to look at has very seldom been read in church. It blows your mind when you read it for the first time. Unending joy flooded my heart as I studied it and saw what it reveals about Jesus and all He has done for us! This passage is flooded with Jesus' work on the cross and confirms our freedom from sin and death. We need to realize that every false interpretation of a passage of Scripture does not only mislead us but also blinds us to its truth. I believe we have to get every form of tithing teaching, that has its aim set on giving money to the church, completely from our minds before making a study on this topic. If we don't do that, we will unknowingly seek for what we already know. The best thing we can ever do is to **ask the Holy Spirit to point us to Jesus in the Scripture**. We need to always see the message of the incarnation, death, and resurrection of Jesus Christ in every Scripture, especially when it comes to laws given to the Israelites.

Let's see if we can find, in these verses, the Trinity dynamics, the union we have with God in Jesus, what He has done for mankind, and how He loves us with regard to the subject of tithing:

Jesus and the Omer of Manna

16*This is the thing which the LORD hath commanded,
Gather of it every man according to his eating, an
omer for every man, according to the number of your
persons; take ye every man for them which are in his
tents.* 17*And the children of Israel did so, and gathered,
some more, some less.* 18*And when they did mete it with
an omer, he that gathered much had nothing over, and
he that gathered little had no lack; they gathered every
man according to his eating* (*KJV*, Exod. 16:16-18).

32*And Moses said, This is the thing which the LORD
commandeth, Fill an omer of it to be kept for your
generations; that they may see the bread wherewith I
have fed you in the wilderness, when I brought you
forth from the land of Egypt.* 33*And Moses said unto
Aaron, Take a pot, and put an omer full of manna
therein, and lay it up before the LORD, to be kept for*

your generations. [34] *As the LORD commanded Moses, so Aaron laid it up before the Testimony, to be kept.* [35] *And the children of Israel did eat manna forty years, until they came to a land inhabited; they did eat manna, until they came unto the borders of the land of Canaan.* [36] *Now an omer is the tenth part of an ephah* (*KJV*, Exod. 16:32-36).

We all know the manna that fell from heaven points to Jesus as the bread of life which was to come. (See John 6) The manna they ate in the desert could not give them life at all. The only manna that could give life is Jesus, the bread from heaven.

It is very interesting that the manna given to every person was an Omer of manna, nothing more and nothing less. Let us see if there is any New Testament significance to an Omer of manna.

Omer

An omer was a tenth of an epha:

"Now an **omer** is the **tenth part** of an ephah" (Exod. 16:36)

The root word from where we find the word **omer**, which is a **tenth** of an ephah, means the following:

'âmar aw-mar'
A primitive root; properly, apparently to heap; figuratively to chastise (as if piling blows); specifically, (as denominative from H6016) to gather grain: - bind sheaves, make merchandise of.

According to the Septuagint, the meaning of an Omer is the following.

G1115

Γολγοθᾶ Golgotha *gol-goth-ah'*
Of Chaldee origin (compare [H1538]); *the skull*; *Golgotha*, a knoll near Jerusalem: - Golgotha.

What God commanded was that the manna given to every man had to be measured by an omer, which was a TITHE of an epha. Prophetically interpreted, this points to the manna (bread of life) that had to be chastised or placed on the skull before it could be eaten.

Jesus called Himself the *bread from heaven*, or the *Manna* (See John 6:25-59).

According to Exodus 16, the manna was kept in a vessel before the Lord, which signifies the chastisement of many blows on Jesus' body. The pot of manna, which was a tithe of an epha of manna, points to the blows the *bread from heaven* would bear on Himself for us.

The tithe is very closely connected to food and has wonderful redemptive truthconnected to it. Whenever the Bible speaks about the tithe, inside the Levitical Order, it points to food that had to be eaten in remembrance of Him. By eating this food, you will have life. By **eating** the bread contained in the cup of suffering, you will not see death but have all curses removed from you:

16This is the thing which the LORD hath commanded, Gather of it every man according to his eating, an omer for every man, according to the number of your persons; take ye every man for them which are in his tents. [17]*And the children of Israel did so, and gathered, some more, some less.*[18]*And when they did mete it with an omer, he that gathered much had nothing over, and he that gathered little had no lack; they gathered every man according to his eating* (*KJV*, Exod. 16:16-18).

The tithe belongs to God. It is very clear that the tithe was not pointing to what *we* had to give *God* but what *God* gave *us*! You could not give your tithe to God; you could **only receive** the tithe and **eat it**! I hope you can see how foolish it would be to take the tithe and try to turn it into giving money to the church. There is no correlation between the two and there will never be! The bread that came from Heaven came inside the measure of chastisement and the place called *skull*, chastised unto food that can give life to those who eat it. The bread that was broken, by the blows it sustained, has to be eaten in order for us to have life. The closest we can come to the tithe is at the communion table, where we eat the manna that fell from Heaven. To us, it is food; to God, it is the provision of life for mankind, through the suffering of His Son.

The tithe was food, pointing to the body of Jesus made available as the bread of heaven for us all:

[22]*You will truly tithe all the increase of your seed that the field brings forth year by year.* [23]*And you will eat before Jehovah your God in the place which He will choose to place His name there, the tithe of your grain, of your wine, and of your oil, and the first-born of your herds and of*

your flocks, so that you may learn to fear Jehovah your
God always. 24 And if the way is too long for you, so that
you are not able to carry it, or if the place is too far from
you, which Jehovah your God will choose to set His name
there, when Jehovah your God has blessed you, 25 then you
will turn it into silver and bind up the silver in your hand,
and will go to the place which Jehovah your God will
choose. 26 And you will pay that silver for whatever your
soul desires, for oxen, or for sheep, or for wine, or for
strong drink, or for whatever your soul desires. And you
will eat there before Jehovah your God, and you will
rejoice, you and your household 27 and the Levite within
your gates, you will not forsake him, for he has no part
nor inheritance with you. 28 At the end of three years you
shall bring forth all the tithe of your increase the same
year, and shall lay it up inside your gates. 29 And the
Levite, because he has no part nor inheritance with you,
and the stranger, and the fatherless, and the widow, who
are inside your gates, shall come, and shall eat and be
satisfied, so that Jehovah your God may bless you in all
the work of your hand which you do. (*MKJV*, Deut. 14:22-29).

This is amazing, is it not? Every time I read this, it blesses me to the utmost—an inner joy accompanied with the word, "WHAT?!" hits my inner man time and again. How can we not smile after we have read this verse!

Let's look at this passage, verse by verse:

"You shall truly tithe all the increase of your seed that the field brings forth year by year" (*KJV*, Deut. 14:22).

People were commanded to tithe of whatever increase the field brought forth, year by year. Not one year was to be skipped, except for the **Year of Jubilee and the Sabbath years.**

The following verse will tell you exactly what to do with the tithe, as we see what the Israelites did with what they put aside every year. **Let's look for Jesus and His accomplished work in these verses**. Let's read the WORD that was before time and was manifested in the incarnation, hidden and yet revealed in these verses! If you seek for the truth, which is the WORD, you will find it:

23 *And thou will eat before the LORD thy God, in the place which he will choose to place his name there, the tithe of thy corn, of thy wine, and of thine oil, and the firstlings of thy herds and of thy flocks; that thou may learn to fear the LORD thy God always* (*KJV*, Deut. 14:23).

Unfortunately, the tithe has been seen by the present-day church as provision for pastors and leaders, instead of **food that the tither eats in remembrance of God**. This is absolute abuse of these passages. If we want to tithe today, we should do it in accordance with the biblical prescriptions, which would not be what God wants us to do since it is all fulfilled and not applicable anymore.

What did the Jews have to do with the tithe? No, your eyes are not playing tricks on you. This is what the Scripture states: you will **eat your tithe** before the Lord your God. Here we can see that the tithe has everything to do with food and eating it yourself. Eating the tithe would then teach you to fear the Lord your God. By eating the tithe of the crop, the people learned to have reverence for God. In Hebrew, the word *learn* means *to be prodded or touched in your inner man through remembrance of how blessed you are*, resulting in reverence for God. So, in eating the tithe, the people were prodded in their hearts to remember how much God had blessed them.

Can you think of something that is set apart for us to eat, which prods our inner man to remembrance and gratitude towards Him? Let's look even deeper into this:

24 *And if the way be too long for thee, so that thou art not*
able to carry it; or if the place be too far from thee, which
the LORD thy God will choose to set his name there, when
the LORD thy God hath blessed thee: 25 *Then shalt thou*
turn it into money, and bind up the money in thine hand,
and shalt go unto the place which the LORD thy God will
choose: (*KJV*, Deut. 14:24, 25)

This is the only place where we can connect money with the tithe. The tithe was sold and the money was taken to the place where the tithe was to be eaten. The money was not given to the priests at all—that would be a violation of the tithing law. Since eating in remembrance of His goodness towards us is what the tithe is all about, it was to be turned into food and eaten by the giver of the tithes. You would be sinning if you were to give your tithe in money form to the priest. It would also be a violation of biblical tithing if you did not eat the tithe yourself:

26 *And thou shalt bestow that money for whatsoever thy*
soul lusteth after, for oxen, or for sheep, or for wine, or
for strong drink, or for whatsoever thy soul desireth: and

thou shalt eat there before the LORD thy God, and thou shalt rejoice, thou, and thine household (*KJV*, Deut. 14:26),

The money shall be used for food and it will be eaten by the giver of the tithes. This is clear and so simple to understand, once you are ready to say *teach me Lord*. It would be foolish for me to expound on a Scripture that basically needs no explanation; the passage is clear. I believe that it was a wonderful thing for the people to tithe. It was wonderful for them to take a portion of their crop, go to a place where all their friends gathered, and have a party in remembrance of how God had blessed them. This remembrance would be much more than just a remembrance of how blessed you are. It was establishing, in the hearts of those who ate it, the truth of how friendly, loving, life-giving and caring God is.

What we can clearly see is that the tithe had to be **what your soul desires**. The tithe is what your soul has always lusted after. Does the passage not say that the tithe money should be spent for whatever your soul lusts after? Can you think of something that the soul of mankind desires? Is it not the love, acceptance, innocence, perfection and union provided for man in Jesus! Is it not Jesus Himself!

27 And the Levite that is within thy gates; thou shalt not forsake him; for he hath no part nor inheritance with thee. 28 At the end of three years thou shalt bring forth all the tithe of thine increase the same year, and shalt lay it up within thy gates: 29 And the Levite, (because he hath no part nor inheritance with thee,) and the stranger, and the fatherless, and the widow, which are within thy gates, will come, and will eat and be satisfied; that the LORD thy God may bless thee in all the work of thine hand which thou doest (*KJV*, Deut. 14:27-29).

What I am about to say is directed towards the erroneous teaching in the church that the tithe belongs to pastors, since pastors were foreshadowed by the Levitical priesthood.

It will be very helpful to read the following passage, in order to understand what the Bible means when it says that the Levite shall not be forsaken (forgotten).

When God divided the land, He divided it without giving any land to the Levites. This way, they could not farm and provide for themselves by their own works, for God told them that He was their inheritance. This was also said to Abraham in Genesis 15. When God tells someone that **He** is their inheritance, He is saying that they will not increase by their own works but by the work of God. This is significant when we connect it to the verse that states that we are a royal priesthood (See 1 Pet 2:9).

Because we are the royal priesthood and have had no field to work for our inheritance, since the law was fulfilled, God will have to provide all that we need to live. God's people have no land, since the law—by which we would normally work to produce fruit—was not dealt to us. The church is a royal priesthood and has no field to work for an inheritance. **Jesus inherited the field** in His incarnation; **He worked the field**, and in the third year **He provided food** to the house of God. (I will soon explain this.) There is so much to say about the interpretation of Old Testament types and shadows that one could actually write a book on the subject. Let's read this verse below to see what it means that the Levite shall not be forsaken:

[17]You may not eat inside your gates the tithe of your grain or of your wine or of your oil, or the first-born of your herds or of your flock, or any of your vows which you vow, or your free-will offerings or the heave offering of your hand.[18]But you must eat them before Jehovah your God in the place which Jehovah your God will choose; you, and your son, and your daughter, and your manservant, and your maidservant, and the Levite within your gates. And you will rejoice before Jehovah your God in all that you put your hand to. [19]Take heed to yourself that you do not forsake the Levite as long as you live on the earth (*NKJV*, Deut. 12:17-19).

Forsaking the Levite simply meant that they were not allowing the Levite to eat with them, when they ate their tithe or free-will offering before the Lord. What it does not mean is that they were disobeying God by not giving the whole tithe to the Levite; God was not in any way requiring that of the people. And this passage has nothing to do with giving money to the church, as some teach.

Some people believe that the Levites in the Old Testament represent the pastors of the New Testament. It is from this Old Covenant principle that many churches lay claim to ten percent of people's money these days. The tithe never belonged to the Levite but to God.

If we agree with the Bible that the tithe must be eaten, and that it belongs to God, we must conclude that the tithe is not what we give God but what He gives us! Can you think of something that belongs to God and is given to man, in order to be eaten by man in remembrance of God? God was saying that the Jews were to put ten percent aside as something that belonged to God. God then gave what belonged to Him as food to be used in rejoicing. Even those who had no inheritance, and had not "worked," could eat of what God provided for them to eat. This clearly points to Jesus and His body that was broken for us.

28*At the end of three years thou shalt bring forth all the tithe of thine increase the same year, and shalt lay it up within thy gates:*
29*And the Levite, (because he hath no part nor inheritance with thee,) and the stranger, and the fatherless, and the widow, which are within thy gates, will come, and will eat and be satisfied; that the LORD thy God may bless thee in all the work of thine hand which thou doest* (*NKJV*, Deut. 14:28, 29).

Look how powerfully The Message Bible states this:

28*At the end of every third year, gather the tithe from all your produce of that year and put it aside in storage.*
29*Keep it in reserve for the Levite who won't get any property or inheritance as you will, and for the foreigner, the orphan, and the widow who live in your neighbourhood. That way they'll have plenty to eat and GOD, your God, will bless you in all your work* (*MSG*, Deut. 14:28, 29).

This is so powerful as it points to Jesus in every way!

At the end of every third year: Jesus was crucified at the end of three years of ministry, was He not?

The Levite, the stranger, the fatherless and widow: Every third year, there will be provision made for all those that **cannot provide for themselves**. Please note that all these people had one thing in common; they had no inheritance (or had lost their inheritance).

Who is the **widow**? Who is the **stranger**? Who is the **fatherless**? Who else but mankind! When we read the message of the prodigal son, we see that he squandered his inheritance. When he was in the other land, he was **fatherless** and a **stranger** (See Luke 15:11-32).

The **widow** speaks of the one who has no husband. This can be understood by reading Rom 7:1-5, which says that we became dead to the law when the law-man died in Jesus, so that now we can be married to another.

When God looked at these people, He was seeing you and me, and He wanted to provide food for us. Every third year this food was placed in the storehouse, enough for all who were in need of food, because they had no inheritance and were unable to provide for themselves by their own works. Is this not a beautiful picture of grace and love! Is this not flooded with life! Is it not bringing the inner AMEN of the spirit-man in you to light!

Every third year, the tithe was exclusively made available for those who could not provide for themselves. If we want to take this and apply it to money in church, we will be completely out of line. This is not to be done in the New Testament at all. These verses are talking about Jesus and what **He** came to do on Earth.

The Dreaded Malachi 3

How would Jesus read Malachi 3? He saw that it was speaking to Him about how He would purify mankind. Malachi was a prophet who was prophesying about **Jesus** and all **He** had to do to bring salvation. Did Jesus not come to fulfill the prophets? Yes He did, which means that Jesus read Malachi as a prophetic instruction for Him to fulfill, in bringing forth salvation. Let's read the intimate voice of the Father to the Son in this passage about our salvation. We will be getting into the mind of Jesus, seeing what He saw, and hearing what He heard from the Father as He read it:

1 Behold, I will send My messenger, and He will clear the way before Me. And Jehovah, whom you seek, will suddenly come to His temple, even the Angel of the Covenant, in whom you delight. Behold, He comes, says Jehovah of Hosts. 2 But who can endure the day of His coming? And who will stand when He appears? For He is like a refiner's fire, and like fuller's soap (*NASB*, Mal. 3:1, 2).

These two verses clearly speak of God's **messenger**, John the Baptist, who would prepare the way for Jesus (See Matt.11:10). We see that Jesus is the **Angel of the Covenant** to come as the one that purifies. And all people will be inneed of His purification:

"All have sinned and fallen short of the glory of God" (*NKJV*, Rom. 3:23).

"If You, Lord, should mark iniquities, O Lord, who could stand?" (*NKJV*, Ps. 130:3).

To take this passage out of its historic interpretation, and prophetic fulfilment in Jesus, would be wrong. There is not even a hint of the local church and monthly provision in this passage. Therefore, trying to prove New Testament giving from this passage should set off some red flags. Why would you want to bend the Scripture to something it is not? Could it be that you have fear in your heart that God will not provide for you? Could it be the result of hearing wrong doctrine for many years?

And He will sit as a refiner and purifier of silver. And He will purify the sons of Levi, and purge them as gold and silver, that they may be offerers of a food offering in righteousness to Jehovah (*ASV*, Mal. 3:3).

As we look a little deeper into this verse, we find that God had a problem with the sons of Levi, for not keeping to the prescriptions of the **food offerings**. What God came to do in Jesus was to bring the food offering in a way that is pleasing to Him. This food offering is then described as the tithe in verse 8, (coming up).

Mal 3:4 *Then shall the offering of Judah and Jerusalem be pleasant unto the LORD, as in the days of old, and as in former years.* (*KJV*)

Again, the food offering is mentioned by the Lord. God would like the offering to be in line with the original intent of the offering and not anything else.

Mal 3:5 And I will come near to you to judgment; and I will be a swift witness against the sorcerers, and against the adulterers, and against false swearers, and against those that oppress the hireling in his wages, the widow, and the fatherless, and that turn aside the stranger from his right, and fear not me, saith the LORD of hosts.

Mal 3:6 For I am the LORD, I change not; therefore ye sons of Jacob are not consumed. (KJV, Mal. 3:5, 6).

God declares that He will come to rule against all the bad that is going on. He is going to cleanse the priesthood of all its hypocrisy and thievery. There is much more to be said about this passage, but it would be unnecessary information and not needed to make the point about Jesus being our tithe. Therefore, I will not go into more detail on what is meant by sorcerers, adulterers and false swearers.

Mal 3:7 Even from the days of your fathers ye are gone away from mine ordinances, and have not kept them. Return unto me, and I will return unto you, saith the LORD of hosts. But ye said, Wherein shall we return? Mal 3:8 Will a man rob God? Yet ye have robbed me. But ye say, Wherein have we robbed thee? In tithes and offerings. (*KJV*, Mal. 3:7, 8)

What God made available every third year, to feed His people, was taken from Him so that He was unable to provide for those who couldn't provide for themselves. What God saw as the manna from Heaven was taken from Him. Suddenly, God saw that He could not provide righteousness for those who couldn't attain to righteousness by their own works.

Mal 3:9 "Ye are cursed with a curse: for ye have robbed me, even this whole nation" (*KJV*, Mal. 3:9).

God declares the nation cursed. He is in a place where He cannot provide food on the third year. Since they took the manna, He cannot give them righteousness as a free gift.

They robbed Him from the tithe. The food the weak needed to eat in remembrance of Him was taken from Him. In type and shadow language, this would spell the removal of Jesus. What a tragedy! What a loss! Thanks be to God that all this is just a shadow and not reality.

Mal 3:10 Bring ye all the tithes into the storehouse, that there may be meat in mine house, and prove me now herewith, saith the LORD of hosts, if I will not open you the windows of heaven, and pour you out a blessing, that there shall not be room enough to receive it. (*KJV*, Mal. 3:10).

To end the shadow and manifest His salvation plan, God gives instruction for the tithe to be brought to the storehouse, so that there can be meat in His house. Who and what would the real tithe be? Who can restore the priesthood to God's original intent?

There is so much to say about Malachi 3:10. The fullness of the work of Jesus is found in it. Let's bring it to the light.

Please remember that this verse was seen by Jesus as instructions for bringing freedom to the people of God. This is not an instruction for the New Testament church to bring money to the local pastor, so that God can bless them a hundred, sixty, or even thirtyfold. When Jesus read Malachi, He saw it as the Father speaking to *Him*, instructing *Him* to make His body available as meat for all who cannot provide the food needed for eternal life by their own works: *My Son, your body is the true manna; it is the full tithe, kept in the cup of suffering. Bring it to those who have no inheritance but You. You are the inheritance of all who cannot provide food for life by their own works. My son, if you bring to these people your body the true meat, they will be blessed and You will be blessed.*

The problem God addresses, in Malachi 3, is the problem of having no MEAT in the storehouse. Did Jesus not say that His flesh is MEAT INDEED? (See John 6:55). Yes, He did, and it is marvelous in our eyes! Jesus is the tithe, the bread contained in the cup of suffering! Jesus is the meat provided for the household of God. Glory to God in the Highest!

The Alpha and the Omega

This part is not to be read as doctrine but can be very interesting. Please note that I don't base what I believe on the concept of the Alpha and Omega phenomenon but the prophetic value of the passage. What I am about to share is only a confirmation of what the passage says in its prophetic authority.

There is a word used many times in the Bible that cannot be pronounced or translated into English. In this word, the first and last letters of the Hebrew alphabet are written next to each other. This word is found all over the Old Covenant writings, and we are going to have a look at its appearing and use in Mal 3:10.

Jesus said that He is the Alpha and the Omega, which has a certain meaning to us in the modern world. We feel uplifted and in awe of Jesus when we sing the song, *You are Alpha and Omega, I worship you my Lord, you are worthy to be praised.* Yet, in Jesus' day, to say *you are the Alpha and the Omega* had a completely different meaning, even blasphemous. In the Hebrew, the words basically have no meaning in and of themselves, and cannot be translated into English, although some tried their hand at it and failed miserably. They failed so completely that the one point of translation totally contradicts the other.

The most astounding thing about the Alpha Omega, in Hebrew, *Aleph Tav*, is that it is the word used thousands of times in the Old Covenant. It is used over seven thousand times, yet almost never translated into English. It has been translated one hundred and eleven times into English, using twelve different words, varying from *what* to *wept;* so we can see there is much more to its meaning than meets the eye. We find that the translators had no idea what the word could mean, contradicting themselves in the translation all the time.

When Jesus said He is the Alpha and the Omega, the Hebrew people would have heard Him say He is the *Aleph* and the *Tav*. The *Aleph* is the first and the *Tav* is the last letter in the Hebrew alphabet, translated into Greek as *Alpha* and *Omega*.

Here is the root from where it is contracted:

אות

'ôth

BDB Definition:
1) sign, signal
1a) a distinguishing mark
1b) banner

1c) remembrance
1d) miraculous sign
1e) omen
1f) warning
2) token, ensign, standard, miracle, proof
Part of Speech: noun feminine

Notice *1e) omen*: an omen is **a sign of a futuristic event**. AMAZING! Jesus is the Alpha and the Omega. This word is also found untranslated in Gen 1:1 where it clearly points to Jesus:

Gen 1:1 In the beginning[H7225] God[H430] created[H1254 (H853)] the heaven[H8064] and the earth.[H776] (KJV)

Can you see the untranslated word? The word (H853), just before "the heavens," is *Aleph Tav*. Hebrew scholars teach that H853 points to God. In this case, the verse would read, "In the beginning God the Aleph and the Tav created …" Since there are no grammar marks in paleo Hebrew, one can assume it is referring to the Messiah and His work in every place the Aleph and Tav show up in the Bible.

With this in mind, let's read Mal 3:10:

Mal 3:10 Bring[H935] ye[(H853)] all[H3605] the tithes[H4643] into[H413] the storehouse,[H1004 H214] that there may be[H1961] meat[H2964] in mine house,[H1004] and prove[H974] me now[H4994] herewith,[H2063] saith[H559] the LORD[H3068] of hosts,[H6635] if[H518] I will not[H3808] open[H6605] you[(H853)] the windows[H699] of heaven,[H8064] and pour you out[H7324] a blessing,[H1293] that[H5704] *there shall* not[H1097] *be room* enough[H1767] *to receive it.* (*KJV*)

Imagine Jesus, knowing He is the Aleph and the Tav, reading this verse. This is how it would read for Jesus:

Bring yourself, Jesus, the tithe in the storehouse, that there might be meat in my house and prove me now herein, if I will not open Jesus, the ***windows*** *of Heaven, and pour out a blessing that there will not be room enough to receive it* (Mal. 3:10).

Is Jesus not the window we have to Heaven? Is Jesus not the manna that we have to eat? Is the body of Jesus not the food in the house of God? Do we not receive freedom when we eat His flesh and drink His blood? Yes! Jesus is the tithe brought into the storehouse—a million times yes! Hallelujah!

And I will rebuke your devourer, and he will not decay the fruit of your ground against you; nor will your vine miscarry against you in the field, says Jehovah of Hosts (*MKJV*, Mal. 3:11).

Now we can also better understand verse 11. And God will rebuke the devourer of the fruit, on account of what Jesus has done. When there is bread and wine in the house of God, when the true manna comes from Heaven and is eaten by the people of God, the people start to bear fruit, and the life of the flesh and its fruit is over. I know this might shock you, but it is simply a confirmation of what is clearly declared in Malachi 3. It could not be understood by Jesus in any other way. I think I have said enough on tithing to help those that want to hear and learn. I think what is said is more than enough to spark a fire in you that will change your life forever. I could go through every verse in the Old Covenant and explain the very thing I have made clear here.

Conclusion:

- The tithe of Abraham was part of the Chaldean system of the time and serves to show us that Jesus has the authority to change the law.
- Jesus was the fulfillment of the type and shadow of the tithe, which is His body, the real bread from Heaven for all who want eternal life to eat by believing in Him.
- Tithing can never be money and has never been taught in the New Testament as giving to the local church. In fact, this has not occurred anywhere in Scripture—not even once.

CHAPTER 13

Did Jesus Say We Should Tithe?

Jesus and the famous *you should not have neglected tithing* **Scripture:**

Woe unto you, scribes and Pharisees, hypocrites! for ye pay tithe of mint and anise and cummin, and have omitted the weightier matters of the law, judgment, mercy, and faith: these ought ye to have done, and not to leave the other undone (*KJV*, Matt. 23:23).

First of all, I would like to tell you what this verse does NOT say:

- It does not say that tithing should be given to the local church.
- It does not say that tithing should continue in the New Testament.

There is no scriptural, historical or contextual evidence that this verse points to giving money to the local church. It has nothing to do with the local church today and everything to do with the Jewish laws in effect at that time. When Jesus was speaking in Matthew 23, the Law and all the sacrifices were still to be fulfilled—especially the tithing and sacrificial laws—since Jesus had not yet died.

The tithe had not yet come to the storehouse, because the body of Jesus had not yet been broken and made available as food for all people. On account of this, they still had to follow the principle described in Deuteronomy 14. Is it not clear in the passage that the people were tithing of food? How did they tithe? They took the mint, anise, and cumin, and ate it at the temple once a year. Every third year they kept it in their cities and the poor, widows, Levites, and strangers ate of it.

Jesus was saying they should be merciful and loving, while eating the tithe as described in the Law. The teachers of the Law, and holy men, kept the Law to the letter; they were tithing as they were supposed to tithe. It would have been seen as the greatest corruption and disobedience to take the tithe, turn it into money, and give the money to the Levite, poor or stranger, for it would be a massive violation of the prescriptions of how one should tithe. That would be seen as not keeping to the Law and one would be found a transgressor of the Law.

Jesus was the meat that would come to the storehouse, so not long after He told them to continue eating the tithe everything would change. Imagine you refuse to stop tithing and you still eat the tithe every year as the Law commanded. Would that not also be against the true tithe that has come? Once the substance has arrived, there is no need for the shadow. This verse is clearly pointing to

Jesus' integrity in the fulfillment of the Law. Jesus did not come to break the Law but to fulfill it. Once the Law is fulfilled, like prophecy, it no longer has value except for the fulfillment right in front of you. Since the manna from Heaven (Jesus) had to be tithed (placed in an omer, which means to be placed on Golgotha and chastised), Jesus would not be against them tithing by eating the mint and spices, since it was still a system that was to be fulfilled by Jesus. Jesus was not referring to tithing as giving money to the priests. It would be erroneous to conclude, from this verse, that Jesus was commanding the New Testament Church to give ten percent of their money to the local congregation. There is not the slightest hint of that in this passage.

Paying tithes according to the prescriptions of the Old Covenant, in the presence of the resurrected Jesus, would be dishonoring the meat that came to the storehouse. It would be seen as dishonoring the work of Jesus on the cross. If we want to tithe today, we should keep in mind that the tithe will be for all the strangers, widows, and priests in town. If we say that the priest is the pastor, then who are the strangers and widows?

The passage in question simply states that it was not wrong for the Pharisees to even eat ten percent of spices and to be very careful in observing the Law to the letter, **while the system was still active**. This type and shadow of tithing was fulfilled when Jesus was chastised and hanging on the cross at Golgotha, providing the real tithe, which is the real meat in the storehouse.

CHAPTER 14

The Right of the Preacher – What is It and How Should It be Implemented?

You need to know that what I am about to say is so far from what we've traditionally heard that you might think I have lost my mind! All I ask is that you hear me out. Very important parts of the passage will be placed in bold:

3 *My answer to those who examine me is this:* 4 *Do we not*
have authority to eat and to drink? 5 *Do we not have*
authority to lead about a sister, a wife, as well as other
apostles, and as the brothers of the Lord do, and Cephas?
6 *Or is it only Barnabas and I who have no authority*
whether not to work? 7 *Who serves as a soldier at his own*
wages at any time? Who plants a vineyard and does not
eat of its fruit? Or who feeds a flock and does not partake
of the milk of the flock? 8 *Do I say these things according*
to man? Or does not the Law say the same also? 9 *For it*
is written in the Law of Moses, "You will not muzzle an
ox threshing grain." Does God take care for oxen? 10 *Or*
does He say it altogether for our sakes? It was written for

us, so that he who plows should plow in hope, and so that he who threshes in hope should be partaker of his hope (*MKJV*, 1Cor. 9:3-10).

In this passage, Paul is taking the common sense of farming and government to explain that it's not wrong for a person who works to be paid. Yet, he is not saying that we should demand money from people and base our demand on certain Scriptures. He is simply explaining the common sense of serving and receiving support for what you have done. The logic is clear: if you work, it is not wrong to eat of the fruit of your labor.

11 If we have sown to you spiritual things, is it a great thing
if we will reap your carnal things? 12 If others have a share
of this authority over you, rather should not we? But we
have not used this authority, but we endured all things lest
we should hinder the gospel of Christ. 13 Do you not know
that those who minister about holy things live of the things
of the temple? And those attending the altar are partakers
with the altar. 14 Even so, the Lord ordained those
announcing the gospel to live from the gospel. 15 But I
have used none of these things, nor have I written these
things that it should be done so to me; for it is good for me
rather to die than that anyone nullify my glorying. 16 For
though I preach the gospel, no glory is to me. For
necessity is laid on me; yea, woe is to me if I do not preach
the gospel! 17 For if I do this thing willingly, I have a
reward; but if against my will, I am entrusted with a
stewardship. 18 What then is my reward? That when I
preach the gospel I may make the gospel of Christ without

charge, that I may not abuse my authority in the gospel (*MKJV*, 1Cor. 9:11-18).

It is clear Paul never thought that he needed to be rewarded with an offering for his preaching. In fact, the real reward, for Paul, was to make the Gospel without charge—free for all. Make the Gospel without charge; this means that Paul did not charge to preach. Charging to preach the Gospel, or demanding giving, would be abuse of one's right as a preacher. We have no right to charge money for our preaching; we only have a right to receive money should people give it freely, so it would not be a hindrance to the Gospel.

19For though I am free from all, yet I have made myself
servant to all, so that I might gain the more. 20And to the
Jews I became as a Jew, so that I might gain the Jews. To
those who are under the Law, I became as under the Law,
so that I might gain those who are under the Law. 21To
those who are outside Law, I became as outside Law (not
being outside Law to God, but under the Law to Christ),
so that I might gain those who are outside Law. 22To the
weak I became as the weak, so that I might gain the weak.
I am made all things to all men, so that I might by all
means save some. 23And this I do for the sake of the
gospel, so that I might be partaker of it with you (*MKJV*,
1Cor. 9:19-23).

What 1Cor. 9:3-23 does NOT say:

- It does not say that because the tithe belongs to God we should take it to the local church.

- It does not say we can demand money from people if we have preached to them.
- It does not say the Abrahamic tithe was still active. (There is not even the slightest hint of that.)
- It does not say today's preacher has all the rights of the Old Testament priest.
- It does not say we can take the old Jewish laws and demand money from people.
- It does not say that we can ask money for preaching the Gospel.
- It does not say the people you preach to should feel burdened to care for you.
- It does not say people will receive more money if they give money.
- It does not say we are allowed to make merchandise of the church.
- It does not say you can expect money from the individual. (We expect our provision from the Gospel, and while that is through the people we minister to, an expectation cannot be placed on the **individual** that he or she MUST give to you. I can expect that I will have provision through preaching, but not expect a **certain** church should give to me when I preach there.)
- It does not say we can make a business of the church, by making preaching our occupation and the church our source of income.
- It does not say the preacher should preach because he needs money, but because of the burning desire God has placed in his heart for people to know the Gospel.

What the passage DOES say:

- It does say that it's not wrong to live off the Gospel as

a preacher.

- It does say that it's not a sin to receive the giving that is **freely given**.
- It does say that one should not muzzle the ox (refuse to allow the preacher to receive from the people, who **want** to give to him from a heart of generosity).
- It does say that it's basic knowledge in law, farming, government, and the Gospel that people can live from what they do.
- It does say we should not be antagonistic towards those who are willing to leave their jobs and live off the free-will giving of the people to whom they minister.
- It does say the concept of receiving, from those who give to you when you preach, is not a man-made concept, but something ordained by God.
- It does say that it can be better not to make use of the right in some instances.

From this passage, we can extrapolate that Paul was under the scrutiny of people who were very money conscious; they were questioning the motive of his preaching. Because they thought Paul should not get any food, lodging, or any form of provision from the people to whom he preached, Paul defends the right of preachers to have material care from the people to whom they minister. The right he is talking about is not in the context of **demanding** provision, but **receiving** on account of the fruit the Gospel brings forth in the believer. When Paul talks about the right to reap material things when spiritual things are sown, it should always be seen in the context of generosity and not demanded giving. What I would like to make clear is that Paul said it was not a big thing if people, from the love of their hearts, give to the preacher that has helped them to see the fruit of the Spirit come forth in their life. Should a preacher's right be exercised, by demanding that the people give to him, it will give place for all kinds of evil, just as the traditional teaching on sowing and reaping, tithing, and seed faith has done.

I am sure people said things like, "Paul only preaches for the money; he goes to towns without having a job. Who does he think must provide for him? Is he expecting the people to take care of him? I am sure he is only in this for the money."

Paul is not saying a preacher has the right to demand money from people because he ministers to them. He is simply saying it is not wrong to receive money or provision from the people to whom you minister. Receiving from those that you minister to is proper, yet it is not the end goal of ministry. We see Paul addressing this in his letter to Timothy, when he states that those who labor in word are worthy of the support they receive. Paul is telling Timothy he should allow support to those who have no other income, on account of giving themselves to the word and teaching.

Let's make that practical. When someone ministers and you are not *muzzling the ox*, you will provide the opportunity for people to follow the generosity in their hearts towards the preacher. This will be all that is needed for the preacher to have enough to live. You should not manipulate and make promises about how God will bless the givers if they give to the preacher; this would be wrong and unbiblical.

Let me put this in even clearer terms: Paul is saying that you cannot demand a car from the people in your church, but if they want to give you one, on account of the word bearing the fruit of generosity in their hearts, you have the right to receive it. Making use of the right you have as a preacher would be to take what they freely give. Not making use of your right, as a preacher, would be to turn it down when they want to give it. Paul expected provision from churches but the expectation was between him and God, not him and the people.

CHAPTER 15

Fruit Abounding to Your Account – Phil 4:19

Paul's expectation, and the perfect application of the right of the preacher, discussed in 1 Corinthians 9, is described in the finest detail in Philippians 4:10-20. Although it should be easy to understand what Paul is talking about in this passage, our traditions have made it difficult for us.

Traditionally, we've interpreted key verses in Philippians 4 to be speaking primarily about money. Along with Phil. 4:19, "My God shall supply all your needs," is the other well-known verse, Phil. 4:13, "I can do all things through Christ." We quote these verses to encourage ourselves to accomplish great things; yet, what we don't know is that Philippians 4 is actually talking about **contentment**. Let's go through this passage, verse by verse, and then connect it to 1 Corinthians 9, in our conclusion on the right of the preacher:

10 But I rejoiced in the Lord greatly, that now at the last your care of me hath flourished again; wherein ye were also careful, but ye lacked opportunity.
11 Not that I speak in respect of want: for I have learned, in whatsoever state

I am, therewith to be content. [12]*I know both how to be abased, and I know how to abound: everywhere and in all things I am instructed both to be full and to be hungry, both to abound and to suffer need.* [13]*I can do all things through Christ which strengtheneth me* (*KJV*, Phil. 4:10-13).

The reason Paul is so happy about how the church, in Philippi, has given to him is that he is glad to see the Gospel bearing fruit in them. He makes very sure that the people understand it's not that he's happy because his need was met. The joy he expresses is on account of the Gospel bearing fruit in them. **This means that he would be just as happy if the money was given to someone else**. The integrity of the Trinity life is astounding; how wonderful that we can have the life of God manifest in us!

Paul explains that Christ has given him the ability to be ***content***, which means *to see no need to add anything to your situation to feel blessed and loved by God.* Paul has no need, because Christ strengthens us to be happy in wealth and in poverty. This is the place where neither wealth nor poverty has any voice. This is what I call being seated in the Trinity, experiencing the Trinity life of the Spirit—the highest quality of life.

Verses 11 to 13 actually state that the poverty in Paul's life did not cause him to think the church should give to him because he preached to them. Paul made sure the people knew he was not secretly, in his heart, demanding money from them. He was genuinely happy in the state he was in—supernaturally happy. The modern-day church has lost this kind of integrity. The traditional teaching of sowing and reaping does not make provision for this kind of integrity, for it is simply too weak to produce this kind of fruit. This kind of holiness can only come forth from the revelation that removes the root of all evil from the heart of a person. This removal happens when we see our union with the Divine Ones, sharing in their quality of life. This kind of life cannot be copied or faked; it can only be born of God.

Some people might hate to hear what I'm saying here, for it might sound as if I am settling for poverty; I am not! I am settling, yes, but only for His abundant life in which true prosperity cannot be defined by any amount of money. Unless we can say from the depth of our hearts that we are rich, while having no money—seeing no need to add anything—we have yet to experience what Paul talks about here. This I don't say condemningly but to bring hope and freedom to you!

"Notwithstanding ye have well done, that ye did communicate with my affliction" (*KJV*, Phil. 4:14).

The way Paul is making use of his right to receive from people, who freely give, is by encouraging them not to interpret what he is saying to mean they have done something wrong by giving to him. WOW! (Let me put this in simple words.) This is what our beloved apostle is telling the church: *I am so happy that you gave. Not that I was desperately waiting for you to do something for me; I am happy just as I am, rich or poor. What makes me happy is to see that the word has entered your heart to the point of bearing fruit. Please don't think I am ungrateful for your giving; it is wonderful and beautiful. I just want you to be sure that I was not demanding this from you. What makes me happy is to see the word working in you, not what I can get from the word working in you. I cannot deny that the word bearing its fruit in you has changed my situation; I am grateful for it. However, the greatest joy in my heart is to see Jesus manifesting in you. This is what it is all about! (Bertie Brits)*

I would like to say this again: Paul is exercising his right, mentioned in 1 Cor. 9. Can you see how he does this with the greatest respect for people? Can you see how he would've even been happy if they had given it to someone else? Paul lives off the Gospel—not the people, although people are involved. Paul lives off the fruit that comes from the Word. He is not making them promises of great wealth, and then benefitting from their giving into his fruitful ministry. There is not even the slightest hint of that.

Now ye Philippians know also, that in the beginning of the gospel, when I departed from Macedonia, no church communicated with me as concerning giving and receiving, but ye only (*KJV*, Phil. 4:15).

Paul says there was no other church from whom he received support but this church. Please note that it would be absolutely wrong to take this verse and build a doctrine of giving, wherein God will make you rich, if you give to the preacher. When we look at 1 Cor. 9, as we connect it to Philippians, where the practical application of the rights mentioned in Corinthians is expressed, we can understand what Paul was saying to the Corinthian church:

16 *For even in Thessalonica ye sent once and again unto*

my necessity. [17]*Not because I desire a gift: but I desire fruit that may abound to your* ***account*** (*KJV*, Phil. 4:16, 17).

The word *account,* in this passage, has been taught as a bank account. It does not mean bank account at all. Here is the Greek meaning:

logos log'-os

From G3004: something said (including the thought); by implication a topic (subject of discourse), also reasoning (the mental faculty) or motive; by extension a computation; specifically (with the article in John) the Divine Expression (that is, Christ):

The word *account* is the word **LOGOS**. Paul is saying that he was not seeking the money but the report or WORD that will go forth about the church. The message (logos) that will go around about the church would be that they are a generous fruitful church. That is what he was seeking. It was not giving that Paul was after, but the WORD having its effect in their lives.

But I have all, and abound: I am full, having received of Epaphroditus the things which were sent from you, an odour of a sweet smell, a sacrifice acceptable, well-pleasing to God (*KJV*, Phil. 4:18).

As members of a church, it is very important to understand that your giving makes a difference in the lives of those for whom you give. Here we can see Paul getting out of a financially difficult situation after the people gave. Let the word dwell richly in your heart unto the bearing of fruit. The bearing of this fruit changes things for us all.

It is not wrong for those who minister the Gospel to receive money from people who want to give to them; it is God-ordained and really makes a difference. So, let's not settle for a fruitless life. Let's allow the word to dwell richly within us unto the bearing of its fruit.

19But my God will supply all your need according to his riches in glory by Christ Jesus. 20Now unto God and our Father be glory for ever and ever. Amen (KJV, Phil. 4:19, 20).

Verse 19 has been so abused that it would be difficult for most to see what it means.

What it does NOT mean:

- It does not mean that God will meet their needs because they gave to Paul.
- It does not mean that God will supply only the needs of the people who gave, excluding those who did not.
- It does not mean that God will meet our needs because we give.

What it DOES say and express:

- It expresses the care Paul had for those who have less because they gave.
- It expresses the foundation from where God supports His people.

- It says that God will meet the needs of people, according to His riches in His glory by Christ Jesus.

Is it not beautiful to see how Paul never loses sight of Trinity logic when he teaches? Can you see how Paul sees the people united with God in Christ? Can you see how he teaches that all their needs will be met inside that glory, which is the goodness of God in the resurrection power? Can you see that Paul is saying their needs will be met by Jesus? Can you see how it would be utterly out of context, and wrong, to conclude that the people's needs will be met by their giving? That is not what this passage suggests at all!

Whenever we assign any attributes to God that will kill the Abba in God, it will always be to our own detriment. Where is the Abba heart of God expressed in a teaching that says, "God will meet your needs only according to your giving"!

In conclusion, we can see that 1 Corinthians 9 tells us it's absolutely normal and right for preachers to receive money from those who want to give, as a result of the word bearing fruit in them. The right of the preacher is not to demand financial support but to receive it, should it be given with a joyful heart.

CHAPTER 16

What about Sowing and Reaping?

The two verses that need our attention in this matter are 2 Corinthians 9 and Galatians 6:6-10. After in-depth study, I have found that the passage in 2 Corinthians 9, which speaks about sowing sparingly and reaping in accordance to what you've sown, has been so drastically taken out of original intent that what the verse actually states becomes difficult to see. This isn't because the verse isn't clear but from the blindness of heart caused by the traditional sowing and reaping teaching.

This is also true for the verse in Galatians 6, where Paul states that God is not mocked; whatever you sow you will reap. The passage does not say if you give sparingly you will reap little amounts of money, and if you give much you will have a lot of money. There is not even a hint of that in the true meaning of either of these passages.

We don't want the death of our Abba, as I shared in Chapter 2, do we? Please prayerfully read through these passages and then let me explain what they are saying. I purposefully copy these large portions of Scripture into the book because I have found that a lot of people don't open the

Bible to read a text that is discussed in a book.

6Let him that is taught in the word communicate unto him that teaches in all good things. 7Be not deceived; God is not mocked: for whatsoever a man soweth, that will he also reap. 8For he that soweth to his flesh will of the flesh reap corruption; but he that soweth to the Spirit will of the Spirit reap life everlasting. 9And let's not be weary in well doing: for in due season we will reap, if we faint not (*KJV*, Gal. 6:6-9).

The context of this passage is false teaching infiltrating the church, preachers visiting the church, support for preachers, and the fruit of wrong doctrine.

Defining *in the flesh*:

2This only I would learn from you: Did you receive the Spirit by works of the law, or by hearing of faith? 3Are you so foolish? Having begun in the Spirit, do you now perfect yourself ***in the flesh****? 4Have you suffered so many things in vain—if indeed it was in vain? 5Then He supplying the Spirit to you and working powerful works in you, is it by works of the law, or by hearing of faith? 6Even as Abraham believed God, and it was counted to him for righteousness. 7Therefore know that those of faith, these are the sons of Abraham* (*KJV*, Gal. 3:2-7).

In those days, there were Jews going around making disciples of the Gentiles (See Matt 23:15), because they believed they needed to be included in the realm that the

Messiah would come to save. They wanted the Gentiles to be a part of the covenant, by baptizing and circumcising them, and giving them the Law of Moses to uphold. By doing this, the Jews believed they qualified the Gentiles to be part of the Messianic reign. These false teachers knew that the promise was only made to those that are children of Abraham. They defined *children of Abraham* as physical descendants who were circumcised. They would also include Gentiles who would repent of sin and idolatry, and become circumcised. Believing this lie is what it means to be *in the flesh.*

The foundation of salvation, according to these false teachers, was not that a person simply believes the Holy Spirit will bring life by the promise of God. Believing that the Holy Spirit will raise you up in the last day and bring forth fruit was not enough for them. When we read chapters 3 to 5 of Galatians, we see Paul explaining that a child of Abraham is not defined by circumcision in the flesh, or physical descent, but by having faith in God. Paul addresses the flesh in most of his writing, according to this definition I have given here.

The fruit of being in this fleshly belief is described in Galatians 3 as *sin* and *all kinds of evil*, which are not part of the inheritance made available for us in Jesus. This kind of life is also described in the Bible as *corruption, decay* and *death.*

It is in light of this background that Paul gives his advice to the church about supporting those who minister the Gospel. If we don't read it this way, we will be missing what Paul is actually saying. Paul believed that it was good both to minister the Gospel and support the preacher.

He told the people to partner with those who teach them. Partnering, in this context, means to support the preacher, by believing what they preach as well as ministering to them through giving, as explained in 1 Cor. 9. **This does not go without a serious warning** by the beloved apostle. The warning he issues is based on the foundation in Galatians 3. He explains that the effect supporting the wrong message and teacher will have on the lives of the believers is **corruption**, which is obviously the opposite of eternal life:

[7]*Be not deceived; God is not mocked: for whatsoever a man soweth, that will he also* ***reap****.* [8]*For he that soweth to his flesh will of the flesh* ***reap*** *corruption; but he that soweth to the Spirit will of the Spirit* ***reap*** *life everlasting* (*KJV*, Gal. 6:7, 8).

The fruit that partners of the wrong message will reap is clearly mentioned in the following passage of Scripture. Read this carefully and see the devastating effects of a mixture 'gospel':

[19]*Now the works of the flesh are clearly revealed, which are: adultery, fornication, uncleanness, lustfulness,* [20]*idolatry, sorcery, hatreds, fightings, jealousies, angers, rivalries, divisions, heresies,* [21]*envyings, murders, drunkennesses, revelings, and things like these; of which I tell you before, as I also said before, that they who do such things will not inherit the Kingdom of God* (*MKJV*, Gal. 5:19-21).

In verses 19 through 21, Paul explains the *reaping* (verses 7 and 8), as the effect the message they support and believe will have on them. He was warning the believers not to mock what God did in Jesus, by adding the law to His work. Mixing the system of circumcision in the flesh with the work of God would simply be a mockery of His love and passion for mankind. Telling a person that he can become part of God's people after he believed the Gospel, expecting the promise of eternal life, according to the Spirit dwelling in him, would be mocking the Spirit of God, rejecting the power of His salvation and life.

It is very clear that this Scripture, in its context, does not teach that the giving of money to a preacher will multiply your money. It actually teaches that giving yourself to the Gospel of the Spirit brings the fruit of the Spirit (mentioned in Chapter 3). It also teaches that you will reap death, should you believe and give yourself for the mixture message that is preached by the false preachers of the **law/grace mixture**. As this is true for death it is true for life. When we support the true Gospel, our heart will be where our treasure is and be flooded with the truth. The truth will then give us immortality (eternal life), should we believe it to the end.

To take this verse, to prove supernatural financial gain because you support a preacher, would simply be incongruent with the concept Paul is actually explaining. As a matter of fact, it would be exactly the opposite. If you think that you can have supernatural wealth, because of the work of giving to an anointed preacher, you are actually in the flesh. This is where a lot of the pain and hurt in church regarding money is rooted.

Let's not mock God with our financial sowing unto prosperity. Does the Scripture not conclude that the birds don't sow or reap? Does it not say that God cares for them, outside of sowing and reaping, and that we are worth more than they? Let's not mock His love by trying to work some principle unto prosperity. All provision is found in ABBA; let that be enough. Let our giving have nothing to do with what we expect God to do for us when we give. The Spirit of God is a Spirit of generosity. Walk in the Spirit and you will be free from stinginess, by the power of the resurrection. Sowing money unto financial prosperity can never set you free from a love for money. It will only worsen the matter.

But this I say, He which soweth sparingly will reap also sparingly; and he which soweth bountifully will reap also bountifully (*KJV*, 2 Cor. 9:6).

The verse you just read is one of the most confusing verses in the Bible; in fact, it is impossible to understand without grasping what we've talked about thus far. We need to understand the dilemma Paul was in, which is described in Chapter 9 of 2 Corinthians. Reading this verse, without understanding all that I have just mentioned, will lead you to believe that your financial blessing can be connected to bountiful giving. This would be a lie and not the truth. This lie will possess the power to grab a hold of the sin, contained in human flesh, that seeks life by works. Death will thrive, as it is engraved into the root of this lie; this will result in all sorts of pain and destruction.

The sad thing about *prosperity by financial giving* is that it is presented "in the name of Jesus." Should this concept be challenged, the person programmed by this wrong belief will think the challenge is satanic. When, in reality, the challenge is coming from the truth of God and His love for us. Thanks be to God that He is greater than our hearts. His word is sharper than any sword and can distribute life, peace and true freedom to us all!

What I am about to explain to you is that the sowing and reaping Paul was talking about was that the church in Corinth would, by grace, fulfill the promise they made a year prior to the letter. I will also explain that Paul was trying to avoid disappointment in the hearts of people. The reaping would be the worship towards God by those in Jerusalem as well as a good report about the church based in Corinth. This good report would be on account of their bountiful generosity towards the poor in Jerusalem. You might think that I am taking a shot in the dark; you might think that it is impossible for the Scripture to actually have this meaning. Let me assure you of this truth, by explaining the history and setting of chapters 8 and 9.

The key verses that everything pivots around are found in Chapters 8 and 9 of 2 Corinthians:

1For as touching the ministering to the saints, it is superfluous for me to write to you: 2For I know the forwardness of your mind, for which I boast of you to them of Macedonia, that Achaia was ready a year ago; and your zeal hath provoked very many. 3Yet have I sent the brethren, lest our boasting of you should be in vain in this behalf; that, as I said, ye may be ready: 4Lest haply if they of Macedonia come with me, and find you unprepared, we (that we say not, ye) should be ashamed in this same confident boasting (*MKJV*, 2 Cor. 9:1-4).

These verses explain the following:

- Paul felt boldness to write to the church in Corinth about giving to the poor. This was because of the Corinthians' willingness to help the poor, on their own initiative.
- Paul boasted to the churches in Macedonia province about what the church in Corinth wanted to do.
- Many other churches were influenced by the willingness of the Corinthians to contribute to the necessity of the poor churches.
- Other churches had their gifts ready about a year earlier, on account of the zeal of the Corinthians about whom Paul boasted.
- The Corinthians had not given what they promised, while others had already given, based on what the Corinthians sparked in them.
- Paul was afraid that some of the poor churches in Macedonia, who gave because of Paul's boasting about the Corinthian church, would travel with Paul to Corinth in order to receive the gifts they promised, then find out that the Corinthians only promised and have nothing to give. This would make Paul's boasting in vain. I can see Paul stressed about this situation. He was very concerned for the churches in Macedonia who gave. They gave in the midst of the deepest poverty. Paul must have thought that this will be absolutely heart breaking for them to see that the people who had the initiative gave nothing in the end, causing discouragement in all those that expected what was promised.
- Paul did not want to be humiliated and did not want to bring humiliation to the Corinthians about this matter.

Let's read the same passage in The Message Bible. I love

reading The Message, not as a true translation from the Greek, but to get the mood and spirit of what was said. We can see the heart of our Abba in Paul. It is wonderful to see that Paul never moves outside of the logic found in the Divine Ones, even when he's between a rock and a hard place. He sticks to the fact that the generosity has to be born in the heart. He does not want to see people humiliated, and above all he does not force them, in any way, as he is constructing a plan to see giving based on grace and not works.

1If I wrote any more on this relief offering for the poor Christians, I'd be repeating myself. 2I know you're on board and ready to go. I've been bragging about you all through Macedonia province, telling them, "Achaia province has been ready to go on this since last year." Your enthusiasm by now has spread to most of them. 3Now I'm sending the brothers to make sure you're ready, as I said you would be, so my bragging won't turn out to be just so much hot air. 4If some Macedonians and I happened to drop in on you and found you weren't prepared, we'd all be pretty red-faced--you and us-- for acting so sure of ourselves. 5So to make sure there will be no slipup, I've recruited these brothers as an advance team to get you and your promised offering all ready before I get there. I want you to have all the time you need to make this offering in your own way. I don't want anything forced or hurried at the last minute (*MSG.*, 2Cor. 9:1-4).

With all of this in mind, we can now go to Chapter 8 and read about what happened in Macedonia, when they heard about the Corinthian initiative to give to the poor churches. The best way for me to explain the passage would be to translate it into simple English, expressing the context and what we have discussed. Ask God to show you the context and what is actually hidden in these verses. It took my heart many years to see the truth in these passages. I knew there was love, compassion, and freedom from legalism hidden in these passages. Here we go:

1 I would like to let you know about the Godly influence
unto generous giving that manifested in the poor churches
in Macedonia. 2 their deepest poverty had no chance to
hold their giving back. The fact that they were so poor yet
so generous on account of the freedom Grace brings
makes this giving simply mind blowing and God ordained.
3 We conclude that what they gave was above what any
person can do by mere human ability. 4 The reason I say it
was God influenced giving is this. They, the poor in
Macedonia, continually begged us to honor them in
allowing them to partaking in giving to the poor. They are
supposed to be on the receiving side, yet Grace liberated
them to see what they have, not focusing or mindful of
what they don't have. 5 We did not go boasting about what
you want to give to the poor in order to get the
Macedonians in on the giving. That was never our motive.
These people gave themselves to God and the Gospel we
preach. This is where it all happened. This grace unto
generosity has its roots in God living in them, not our
hinting by testifying of what you are willing to do. 6 We are
sending Titus to you in order to see the completion of the
very same grace that sparked a willingness to give in you.
You were the first people that experienced this. The word

of His grace manifesting generosity in you, sparked the
same generosity in others all over the region. 7We see the
fruit of the word, the righteousness that flows from the
faith you have, the passion of God and you love in full
manifestation. What we would like to see added to that is
the manifestation and completion of this grace that we
know is in you. 8I'm not trying to order you around
against your will. But by bringing in the Macedonians'
enthusiasm as a stimulus to the love you already have, I
am hoping to bring the best out of you. 9You are familiar
with the generosity of our Master, Jesus Christ. Rich as he
was, he gave it all away for us--in one stroke, He became
poor and we became rich.10So here's what I think: The best
thing you can do right now is to finish what you started last
year and not let those good intentions grow stale. 11Your
heart's been full of this grace giving all along. Follow
your heart unto actually giving.12Once the commitment
is clear, and it is clear in you, you do what you can, not
what you can't. Let the willingness of the heart regulate
your giving.13We are not trying to make other rich by your
giving. The only thing that is going to happen is that the
need they have of food will be met as well as the need you
have as pertaining to giving. 14This concept is even
mentioned in scripture. "there are those that gather all the
time, rich in everything yet their life is poor concerning
giving. There are those that give and still have enough to
live - rich on both sides". Be rich in your giving as you
are in your possessions. Live a well-balanced life, since
the inner willingness is already present with you (MSG., 2
Cor. 8:1-14).

With the foundation firmly established in the context of

these passages, we can now look at those seemingly impossible to understand, highly abused verses in Chapter 9. The key verses that reveal what it is, exactly, that a person will bountifully reap are verses 8-10. By studying these verses, it is clear that Paul is not concerned about financial increase, in the life of the Corinthian Church, but the increase of the fruit of generosity. This is exactly what these verses point to:

And God is able to make all grace ***abound*** *toward you; that ye, always having all sufficiency in all things, may abound to every good work* (*KJV*, 2 Cor. 9:8):

The *abounding* is in good works.

9*As it is written, 'He hath dispersed abroad; he hath given*
to the poor: his righteousness remaineth for ever." 10*Now*
he that ministereth seed to the sower both minister bread for your food, and multiply your seed sown, and increase the fruits of your righteousness (*KJV*, 2 Cor. 9:9, 10);

What is it that will increase through their giving? The fruit of righteousness. What will remain forever, wherein they will be enriched? In the righteous act of giving. The righteousness (giving) of a generous man is not forgotten but remembered.

Paul uses a passage that speaks about the transition grain goes through. Grain is sown, yet it becomes food for those who eat it. Substance for the needs of the poor will be given, and what they will reap is the report of generosity and gratefulness, expressed in worship towards God by the receiver. The increase will not be in money but the effect their righteous act will have on the people on the receiving end. This is very clear in the following verses, which are of utmost importance because they explain what people will reap when they give:

[11]*Being enriched in everything to all bountifulness, which causeth through us thanksgiving to God.* [12]*For the administration of this service not only supplieth the want of the saints, but is abundant also by many thanksgivings unto God* (*KJV*, 2Cor. 9:11, 12);

In conclusion, Paul addresses the church in Corinth that was rich in word, rich in faith, and rich in willingness to give, yet poor in the good work of actually being generous. He is showing them **how to reap a good report** from those people who are about to receive the gift they promised, together with Paul. Paul also knows that there will not be any grudges in the hearts of the Macedonians traveling with him, when they see the church in Corinth generously fulfilling their promise. Paul also reveals how those that are on the receiving end of this generous giving will praise God for what the Corinthians did. I hope your heart can see that the bountiful reaping is a good report and not money. Giving is multiplied and transformed into, "fruit behind the name," as well as praise in the mouths of those that receive it.

What about "pressed down shaken together running over"?

[35]*But love ye your enemies, and do good, and lend, hoping for nothing again; and your reward will be great, and ye will be the children of the Highest: for he is kind unto the unthankful and to the evil.* [36]*Be ye therefore*

merciful, as your Father also is merciful. [37]*Judge not, and ye will not be judged: condemn not, and ye will not be condemned: forgive, and ye will be forgiven:* [38] *Give, and it will be given unto you; good measure,* ***pressed down, and shaken together, and running over****, will men give into your bosom. For with the same measure that ye mete withal it will be measured to you again* (*NKJV*, Luke 6:35-38).

What this passage does NOT say:

- It does not state that giving is the way you activate God's giving to you.
- It does not state that God will judge you if you do not give.

I would like to quote Albert Barnes, a nineteenth century theologian and author of *Notes on the New Testament*. I believe there is not much more to say than what he summarized in his commentary on this passage of Scripture:

Shall men give - This is said to be the reward of "giving" to the poor and needy; and the meaning is that the man who is liberal will find others liberal to him in dealing with them, and when he is also in circumstances of want. A man who is himself kind to the poor - who has that "character" established - will find many who are ready to help "him" abundantly when he is in want. He that is parsimonious, close, [beggarly], will find few or none who will aid him. - **Albert Barnes**

Into your bosom - That is, to you. The word "bosom" here

has reference to a custom among Oriental nations of making the bosom or front part of their garments large, so that articles could be carried in them, answering the purpose of our pockets. **Albert Barnes**

This passage talks about good relationship and unity among people, which is also true for our relationship with God. God did not come judging, hating and abusing us. He showed His love to us; from that platform people loved Him back. In the same way, people will love us when we don't judge them, are good to them, and love them.

This passage is revealing who our heavenly Father is, not giving advice on how to get rich. If we use this verse as a principle to get rich or blessed, we are missing the point of the Scripture. Jesus explains that we have a Father who does not have any hidden agenda. He does not give to get; He does not expect money back, and He loves those who hate Him. The power to save us is in this powerful way of life. What will save us from hatred? A God who loves us and does not hate us. What will set us free from judging? A God who does not judge us. What will restore man's love for his neighbour? Our loving Father.

Luke 6:35-38 points to something much deeper than provision. You will receive what money cannot buy. We need to know that the giving discussed in the New Testament is about not expecting money back; yet, the Scripture states that we will have a reward. What will this reward be? The reward will be the joy of living in the extravagant love of God and seeing that same joy in others, when they are not condemned but forgiven by you. It cannot be excluded that people will naturally do unto you as you do unto them, as explained in the Barnes commentary.

There is something that I believe can be added into the mix. What I am about to say can be seen as a bit of a stretch, yet it is not impossible. Read this next passage with me:

22And it came to pass, that the beggar died, and was carried by the angels into Abraham's bosom: the rich man also died, and was buried; 23And in hell he lift up his eyes, being in torments, and seeth Abraham afar off, and Lazarus in his bosom (*KJV*, Luke 16:22, 23).

The *bosom of Abraham* speaks of the heart of Abraham. The beggar was carried to the place where those who had the heart of Abraham were taken. Why was it not called Heaven? Why was it called the *bosom*?

People will Enter the Heart We Have as They Receive the Love We Give

Just as the poor man was carried *into Abraham's bosom*, when we give, people will give into our bosom. This giving will be on account of the effect love has on people. What I see in this is that people will enter the heart we have as they receive the love we give. They will give themselves into the heart that is expressed in our giving and love. This is the greatest reward and the highest form of life there can ever be! It is a life equal to the life shared in the Divine Ones.

It was out of the passion for having others enter the *bosom* (heart or Spirit of life), that God made people. God made mankind lovable as well as able to love from being loved. The ability to love is born from receiving love. This is how we enter the heart of God, by Him loving us. It is out of God's passion to have people, exactly like Him, inside His bosom (heart) that He loves on them and is good to them. God's hope that we will co-share in His bosom is born from His perception of our value and beauty. When this happens, we share in His quality of life, co-living with God as His friends. I believe this is why Jesus said that it is better to give than receive (See Acts 20:35); not because the giver will have more money but because of what it means to share in the life of God.

Unfortunately, the verse in Luke 6:38 was used to fuel a love for money and not set people free. Remember, the context is not to expect anything back, because we realize that we are not lacking anything. We saw, in our previous discussion, how Paul explained the practicality of this principle in his letter to the church in Corinth. The zeal of the Corinthians made the other churches give into their bosom (heart), by also having a passion to give to the poor. On the other side, we also see that the Corinthian church would be held in high esteem, and fruit added to their bosom. When I say *fruit*, I mean the fruit of generosity that they were actually lacking. Their giving would also multiply in praises to God from the poor who would receive their gifts.

What about "faithful in little and faithful in much..."?

In order to easily understand this passage in our discussion here, you can first go to our Dynamic Love Ministries' website and listen to my message titled, *The UNJUST Steward in the Light of Grace and Not Giving*. Just type "The Unjust" into the search, and this message will appear in the dropdown list. Listening first to it will give you a wonderful foundation from where you can understand what Jesus said in Luke 16. It will also be very helpful to refresh your mind on the emphasis Jews placed on money, by reading Chapter 4 again. In most churches, Luke 16 was never really understood. There are certain things that are simply taboo to talk about in church. Out of fear of addressing taboo topics, and the fear of being labelled, we struggle to see what is actually written in Luke 16.

As we look at this passage, we will have to get a bit over the line and discuss some of the taboo topics. As an introduction to this topic, I would like you to know that I am not against the Jewish people. I am grateful for the Jews, and I love what God has brought through them to us all. I don't believe that God has cast the Jews away. The Jewish people have opportunity to be saved, should they believe in Jesus.

I am fully against the oppression of any nation, including oppression of the Jews. I might differ with the mainstream view on how the Jews will be saved, but I believe it is not of importance in this discussion. As long as you know that God loves all people, including the Jewish people, and that I believe it from the depth of my heart, you will understand the point I am making about this passage.

I also would like you to know that I am not against giving to the local church, nor am I in rebellion against the system that has abused so many. Rebellion against abuse does not equal grace. Let me say that again: rebellion against the system that abused and hurt people cannot be called *grace*.

I am absolutely for generosity and freedom. God has come to give us freedom from pain, hurt and all the forms of the fruit of the flesh, including stinginess. God came to set us free from stinginess by taking away its power, called *the law of sin and death*: "For the law of the Spirit of life in Christ Jesus has made me free from *the law of sin and death*" (*NKJV*, Rom. 8:2). The longer we squabble in the law the longer we will sit in the death of the flesh. I say what I say in order to set people free—not because I am against anybody.

10 He that is faithful in that which is least is faithful also
in much: and he that is unjust in the least is unjust also in
much. 11 If therefore ye have not been faithful in the
unrighteous mammon, who will commit to your trust the
true riches? 12 And if ye have not been faithful in that
which is another man's, who will give you that which is
your own? (*KJV*, Luke 16:10-12)

This passage has been seen as teaching the local church to be faithful in their giving, in order to receive a better revelation, experience more anointing, enter a higher level and have the true riches from God. Although not commonly taught, it has also been taught that giving to the poor assures you a place in Heaven, where you will see all those who will welcome you on account of your giving. Before we read Luke 16, we need to have the thought that *this is Jesus' teaching on giving in the local church* completely removed from our minds. This passage has absolutely nothing to do with giving in the local church at all, not even in the slightest way.

Please remember that Jesus spoke these things while in the process of fulfilling the Law. The Law was not yet fulfilled, the Church was not even born, and the Jewish system was still alive and well to a certain degree. This was not a teaching for church leaders at all. Jesus was addressing the Jewish system and how inadequate it is to save. Luke 16 is actually advice to the Jews on how to get saved, after the stewardship of handling the oracles of God is removed from them. This passage does not address faithful giving in the church in any form or fashion at all.

The passage flows from Luke 15, where Jesus is explaining to them why He is a friend of sinners and tax collectors. Jesus was preaching the Good News to those who were seen as indebted to God on account of some form of sin. The passage has very little to do with money. The only connection it has to money is in what the Jews believed about money, according to Deut. 28.

Let's walk through Luke 16, verse by verse, and come to its Good News conclusion:

And he said also unto his disciples, There was a certain rich man, which had a steward; and the same was accused unto him that he had wasted his goods (*KJV*, Luke 16:1).

What is important to see in this passage is that the rich man (in this case, pointing to God), had goods of His own and a steward had to manage the goods belonging to Him. The goods never belonged to the steward at all. It's what is referred to as "another man's," according to verse 12. The oracles of God were committed to the Jews, according to Romans 3:2. They were the stewards of the message preached to them through Moses and all the prophets.

The message the Jews received is what we call *the law*

system today. The passage in Luke 16 has the same message as the one in Matthew 21:33-44. Look at verse 43:

Therefore say I unto you, The Kingdom of God will be taken from you, and given to a nation bringing forth the fruits thereof (*KJV*, Matt. 21:43).

Jesus is speaking to the Jewish people, telling them that they handled the law incorrectly. They benefited themselves to the point that Jesus is taking the stewardship from them.

- The Jews failed by unbelief in what the law was and to whom it was written.

They failed to present the law as a system that cannot give life, where they would await a Savior who could free them from sin and death. Instead of seeing the law as something that condemns them, and that cannot give life, they embraced it as the way of life. They even called the law *the way, the truth, and the life*. Although the Scriptures were pointing to Jesus, they read it in a way that excluded Jesus, making themselves bad stewards of the law system. They took the law as a commandment written for them to fulfill, thus making themselves a special people with special knowledge. The Jewish people found their identity in the blessings of the law system. They looked down on the poor and regarded the Gentile as a mere dog or a pig.

- They removed the law from the one it was written to.

We need to understand that the law was actually

written to Jesus and not the Jews. Certainly, it was written for the Jews, but only as the power to show them their need for a Savior. It was written especially to Jesus, as the way by which Salvation should come to all mankind.

When we read Psalm 40, we see Jesus explicitly stating that God never required sacrifices but that the Scripture is speaking about Him. The law was never written for the Jews so that by it they could find life. It was a law that belonged to another man. It belonged to Jesus and was written to Him. When Jesus met all the requirements of the law and so fulfilled it, by being the lamb, being the scapegoat, and being the tithe, man was redeemed! Salvation was made available to all people by Jesus fulfilling the law, which was written to HIM.

Whoever removes the law from the opportunity to be fulfilled by Jesus is an unjust steward in how they are handling what is actually written to Jesus. The Jews—and anyone to this day who says that the law is written for people to fulfill—are unfaithful in what is another man's law; they are taking it from the one it belongs to: Jesus!

And he called him, and said unto him, How is it that I hear this of thee? give an account of thy stewardship; for thou mayest be no longer steward (*KJV*, Luke 16:2).

I believe this is talking about the stewardship of the Jews being taken away from them. It signifies the ending of the Levitical priesthood and the manifestation of the Kingdom of God.

3 *Then the steward said within himself, What will I do? for*

my lord taketh away from me the stewardship: I cannot dig; to beg I am ashamed. [4]*I am resolved what to do, that, when I am put out of the stewardship, they may receive me into their houses* (*KJV*, Luke 16:3, 4).

The steward comes to the realization that he is no steward anymore and is not willing to find life by working or begging. I see this to mean that one cannot be saved by works and refuse—by will power or living in denial—to live under the curse. This is the revelation that Jesus would love the Jews to come to. He is lovingly pointing them to the way of life, by explaining to them how—even if they were unjust—they could be commended for walking in true wisdom. Shall the unfaithfulness of man annul the faithfulness of God? No!

Because of the faithfulness of God, the Jews, just as all other nations, have always had Jesus as the Way of Salvation. Why would God exclude the Jews from Salvation through Jesus, just because they handled the shadow wrongly? He will never exclude them from Salvation through faith in Jesus! The true wisdom is revealed in the next verses:

[5]*So he called every one of his lord's debtors unto him, and said unto the first, How much owest thou unto my lord?*
[6]*And he said, An hundred measures of oil. And he said unto him, Take thy bill, and sit down quickly, and write fifty.*
[7]*Then said he to another, And how much owest thou? And he said, An hundred measures of wheat. And he said unto him, Take thy bill, and write fourscore* (*KJV*, Luke 16:5-7).

We need to understand that Jesus was telling this story in light of His love for sinners and forgiveness of sins. The Kingdom of God is a kingdom wherein financial wealth is not a sign of acceptance from God for a person's obedience.

The Kingdom of God is not the same as the kingdom the Jews lived in. They lived in what I call the *Deuteronomy 28 Kingdom*. The Deuteronomy 28 Kingdom is a kingdom where your acceptance is affirmed by financial blessing and all kinds of prosperity. The Kingdom of God is earmarked as preaching the GOOD NEWS of acceptance to the poor.

The poor, sick and suffering people of the Old Testament were living under the constant rejection and disapproval of the voice that money had over them. In their poverty, they heard money's word of judgment over them continually, resulting in the deepest, most painful rejection that man can ever be exposed to, the rejection of their God and Maker. Along with the voice of rejection echoing in the depth of their emptiness and pain, just as loudly they had to hear money speaking of God's acceptance of the rich, the very people who were enforcing the hatred they believed God had for the "disobedient" poor people. The Deuteronomy 28 blessed-by-God, wealthy people looked down on the poor and saw them as cursed by God. They would never befriend the less fortunate, because God's rejection of them seemed obvious—they were poor!

Jesus came preaching the Good News of acceptance to all who were considered, by the old system, to be guilty and rejected. He loved the poor and spent time with them.

When John the Baptist asked if Jesus was the one to come, Jesus replied, "the poor have the Gospel preached to them" (Matt. 11:5), declaring the new and everlasting way of doing things. To preach the Gospel to the poor would be unthinkable in the mind of the Jew. It would be a complete abandonment of everything they believed and stood for. It would be such a radical new way of doing things that Jesus used it as a sign of the coming of the Messiah.

And the lord commended the unjust steward, because he had done wisely: for the children of this world are in their generation wiser than the ***children of light*** (*KJV*, Luke 16:8).

The *children of the light*, in this passage, does not refer to the Church but to the Jews, who considered themselves to be a light to those who walked in darkness and a guide to the blind (See Rom. 2:19). This Scripture, wrongly interpreted, will leave the Church with an underlying feeling of stupidity when it comes to the world. In the true context of the passage, you'll see Jesus was actually teaching that those who didn't make their judgment according to the legalistic system were much wiser that those who strictly stuck to the law-code as a way of life.

And I say unto you, Make to yourselves friends of the mammon of unrighteousness; hat, when ye fail, they may receive you into everlasting habitations (*KJV*, Luke 16:9).

The habitation in which the Jews lived was only temporal, not eternal. The old system was to pass away, never to return. As Jesus is telling them that their habitation is only temporal, He also points them to the eternal habitation which is where those who live by faith, and not works, reside. Here is the wisdom Jesus gave them: Jesus was encouraging them to befriend those whom they thought to be cursed, for the sinners (according to the Jewish system) would enter the kingdom before the Jews, who stuck to the law.

They were to write off the debt of those whom they knew were indebted to the master. By seeing others' debt taken away, they could also enter the place where they would have no debt themselves. The removal of the debt is not measured in money but in what they believed poverty and sickness declared over the poor and the Gentiles. The debt was what they believed the poor and the sick owed God. Jesus came as the perfect example of the forgiveness of debts. He declared the sick forgiven and He healed them; then, they entered the place of having no debt. Jesus saw them as debt-free. That is why He declared them **forgiven**. By healing them, He revealed that He was carrying their sins.

There are some very interesting hidden truths in this passage. How much did the debtors owe the master? A hundred measures of oil and a hundred measures of wheat, right? Interestingly, the oil and the wheat are specifically mentioned in Deuteronomy 14, as what was to be eaten when they ate the tithe:

Deu 14:23 And thou shalt eat before the LORD thy God, in the place which he shall choose to place his name there, the tithe of thy ***corn****, of thy wine, and of thine* ***oil****, and the firstlings of thy herds and of thy flocks; that thou mayest learn to fear the LORD thy God always (KJV).*

What every man actually owed the master is oil and grain.

Oil speaks of the Spirit of God and *corn* (grain) speaks of the body of Jesus. The number 100 also signifies fullness or completeness. All had to have the fullness of Jesus before they could have no debt. The debt they had was a perfect debt that no man could ever pay. The unjust steward then told the man with the oil to sit down (signifying rest), and write *fifty*. The number 50 is a very special number, speaking about the Year of Jubilee, when there would be no debt and all that was lost would be returned to the original owners. It is the *acceptable year of the Lord*, declared by Jesus in Luke 4:16. Instead of debt, declare jubilee. Fifty can also mean 5x10, where 5 = grace and 10 = perfection: perfect grace!

The unjust steward told the one man to write *eighty* measures of wheat. The number 80, according to the Hebrew alphabet, is the letter *Pey*; it means WORD. Instead of debt, give them the WORD. Eighty can also mean 8x10, where 8 = salvation or new beginning, and 10 = perfection. Instead of debt, declare to them Salvation perfected, the new beginning!

Make Friends of the Mammon of Unrighteousness.

What Jesus said here is very powerful. It is clearly seen in the context of all that has already been said. To *make friends of the mammon of unrighteousness* is to write off the debt that is declared over people on account of the law system, where they are found guilty, lacking and wanting off. What Jesus is telling the Jews is that they should realize that the time of their stewardship is drawing to an end. What they should do is to see the mammon system they believe in as unrighteous, and in so doing, they will have room with those who have an eternal habitation and not a temporal one.

I know I am about to repeat myself, but it needs to be understood so that you can enjoy the truth hidden in this passage. The Jews only had a temporal habitation, as stewards of the law and prophetic words God had given them. The law is a temporal habitation, while the bosom of Abraham, which is righteousness by faith, is eternal. If the Jews could realize that their system is one of death and ending, accept the voice of the Jewish money system as unrighteous, and embrace the message contained in the heart of Abraham, they will be saved.

We need to see that the passage has very little to do with money but everything to do with the voice money had in the Jewish system. Jesus is showing the Jews that they were as unfaithful with entrusting what God gave them, in regard to the law and the covenants, as an unjust financial steward would be in finances; they enriched themselves and no one else.

[21]Looking at him, Jesus felt a love for him and said to him, "One thing you lack: go and sell all you possess and give to the poor, and you will have treasure in heaven; and come, follow Me." [22]But at these words [a]he was saddened, and he went away grieving, for he was one who owned much property (*NKJV*, Mark 10:21, 22).

Jesus said the following to him: Find no value in the fact that you are rich, according to Deuteronomy 28. Give to the poor, also, the value that the law would ascribe to the rich and come follow Me. This is how you make friends of the mammon of unrighteousness and in no other way. See people as God sees them on account of what I have done.

Step out of the Jewish law system, and see all people in the light of forgiveness and original design.

10*He that is faithful in that which is least is faithful also in much: and he that is unjust in the least is unjust also in*
much. 11*If therefore ye have not been faithful in the unrighteous mammon, who will commit to your trust the*
true riches? 12*And if ye have not been faithful in that which is another man's, who will give you that which is your own?* (*KJV*, Luke 16:10-12).

We can also say it this way:

Jesus, "If you were caught as unfaithful; if you Jewish people are the unfaithful steward, who will give you the true riches? If the law master you worked for declares you unfit, who will bless you if you stick to him? If you lost your stewardship, there is nothing left for you there. You need to look for life in another place."

No servant can serve two masters: for either he will hate the one, and love the other; or else he will hold to the one, and despise the other. Ye cannot ***serve*** *God and* ***mammon*** (*KJV*, Luke 16:13).

If we look at Luke 16:13, alongside Matthew 6:22-24, we can conclude that to *serve mammon* is to have an evil eye.

22*The light of the body is the eye. Therefore if your eye is*
sound, your whole body will be full of light. 23*But if your* ***eye is evil****, your whole body will be full of darkness. If therefore the light that is in you is darkness, how great is*
that darkness! 24*No one can serve two masters. For*

either he will hate the one and love the other, or else he will hold to the one and despise the other. You cannot ***serve*** *God and* **mammon** (*MKJV*, Matt. 6:22-24).

Can you see how Jesus connects the way you see things with mammon? The *evil eye* Jesus is talking about is not what we give someone when we are displeased with their behavior. The word ***evil*** means *full of labour and overburdened with toil.*

Eye speaks of *a perception, a way of looking and interpreting actions or events*. Serving God and money means to serve God and also serve the system wherein what you achieve by your own works in this life, is life to you.

19 There was a certain rich man, which was clothed in purple and fine linen, and fared sumptuously every day:
20 And there was a certain beggar named Lazarus, which was laid at his gate, full of sores, (the meaning of the Name Lazarus comes from the Hebrew name God of Help
or the God that aids) 21 And desiring to be fed with the crumbs which fell from the rich man's table: moreover the
dogs came and licked his sores. 22 And it came to pass, that the beggar died, and was carried by the angels into Abraham's bosom: the rich man also died, and was
buried; 23 And in hell he lift up his eyes, being in torments, and eeth Abraham afar off, and Lazarus in his bosom.
24 And he cried and said, Father Abraham, have mercy on me, and send Lazarus, that he may dip the tip of his finger in water, and cool my tongue; for I am tormented in this
flame. 25 But Abraham said, Son, remember that thou in thy lifetime receivedst thy good things, and likewise

Lazarus evil things: but now he is comforted, and thou art tormented (*KJV*, Luke 16:19-25).

Jesus is telling the Jews that blessedness, according to the law system, does not equal Salvation. Jesus is telling them that, even with all the blessings of Deuteronomy 28 manifesting in their lives, that can never be a sign of Salvation. Even with all the blessings they received as the Jewish people, they are not free from sin and death. They received the promises, the covenants, and all the oracles of God, yet while being rich in all the dealings God had with them, they remain lost in sin and death. Like all people, they are in need of a Savior. When given the prophetic words of what God will do for all nations, the Jews used those promises to enrich only themselves. They were not a blessing to the nations at all. At best, they were bad stewards of what belonged to Jesus. They were bad stewards of the types, shadows and prophetic words of Salvation for all nations.

26*And beside all this, between us and you there is a great gulf fixed: so that they which would pass from hence to you cannot; neither can they pass to us, that would come from thence.* 27*Then he said, I pray thee therefore, father, that thou would send him to my father's house:* 28*For I have five brethren; that he may testify unto them, lest they also come into this place of torment* (*KJV*, Luke 16:26-28).

Five brothers? Who is it whom Jesus says has *five brothers*? He is the *certain rich man*, from Luke 16:19, who is *clothed in purple and fine linen* (See above). What can all these things mean? There is great truth hidden in the finer details of this passage.

When we look at the twelve tribes of Israel, we find that Jacob had six sons with Leah. This fits perfectly into the story Jesus was telling. Judah, the kingly tribe, and even Levi, from where the Levitical priests were taken, is in this group of Jacob and Leah's six sons. The rich man was dressed in purple and fine linen. He also *fared sumptuously every day.* The purple and fine linen signify the kingly tribe, dressed in the righteousness of the law system. The way they fared speaks of what they ate most of the time; they had tables stacked with the best foods.

"And David said, 'Let their table become for a snare and a trap'" (*MKJV*, Rom. 11:9).

Jesus was telling the Jews that even though they see themselves as rich, according to the law, they would enter death. He was telling them that the system they were part of was going to die and have nothing in it forever. Jesus was saying that the priestly, kingly system they had was a dying system that has nothing in it anymore. There is One of higher kingly order and a different priesthood who has come onto the scene now. His name is Jesus and He is according to the higher order of Melchizedek.

Since the law system is the *ministration of death written on stones* (See 2Cor. 3:7), it will always end in eternal death for those who follow it. Jesus was lovingly warning the Jews to get out of the belief system they have and start to see Jesus as the Messiah.

29 Abraham saith unto him, They have Moses and the prophets; let them hear them. 30 And he said, Nay, father

Abraham: but if one went unto them from the dead, they will repent. [31]*And he said unto him, If they hear not Moses and the prophets, neither will they be persuaded, though one rose from the dead* (*KJV*, Luke 16:29-31).

The rich man tried to cross the gulf between law and grace, by trying to bring the law system into the system of grace. We can clearly hear the voice of Satan in what he says, "If you can raise a man from the dead then all these tribes of Israel will believe in you." This sounds as harmless as, "If you are the Son of God, turn these stones into bread" (See Matt. 4:3). The rich man was actually saying the following: "If you can prove that the message of grace and love can make a person immortal, all of Israel will believe" (See Lk. 16:30).

The answer Abraham gave was exactly what Jesus gave Satan in the desert: you will not have life by what you can perform but by what comes from the mouth of God. If they cannot find life by what is written, they will never have life. There is still much to say about this parable, told by Jesus, but I think this will say enough about the fact that Jesus was not addressing tithing, sowing and reaping, or giving in the local church.

What about "**what about**"?

There are many other passages in the Bible that are used in an attempt to convince people they must give to get God to give to them. They can each be explained, verse by verse, but I am not going to do that. The reason for that is simple: revelation is not hidden in every verse being explained to all people but in a willing heart to learn and know the truth. Pray, asking God to reveal the truth about

His grace to you in every passage you read. What you have received in this book is more than enough to be the second and third mouth confirming the message of God to you, concerning this matter.

CHAPTER 17

A Word of Advice and Encouragement to Church Leaders

God's number one vision for you is not ministry but friendship with Him. As preachers, we can so easily feel unsuccessful if people don't get saved, walk in the power of God and bear fruit. On the other hand, we so quickly feel success when people follow our ministries, give their money and live in obedience to what we preach. We feel so flooded with the satisfaction that 'it is working,' when our church is fast growing. This way of living is not what God intended for you. It will make ministry a living hell for you and for anyone else who believes as you do, and looks to you.

Ask God to show you His love for you. As He shares this with you, just enjoy it. Don't start to put it into a message, thanking God that you have something to preach on the next Sunday.

Most of us went into ministry on account of His passion driving us. Most of us think back to the days when we had pure motives in preaching the Gospel, and we long for those days. Forget those days! They are gone and will never return. Look at Jesus loving you today; don't try to get back to the radical preacher you were when you were young. There is no joy in performance, there is only joy in knowing Him. There is only joy in knowing that He knows you, likes you and loves you.

Remember you are His son, not His preacher. You are a son who also preaches. You are not a preacher who happens to be a child of God.

Enjoying ministry is not found in the outbreak of revival in your church. It is found in seeing **yourself** revived in the resurrection of Jesus, forever one with God. You will enjoy ministry when you are seeing **yourself** seated in the Godhead. Please know that the Gospel of His love is not only for your people but for you also. Believe the Gospel as if you are included in the message.

This chapter is not written to bring you peace, by giving you a grace method by which you can assure yourself that your people will give. The encouragement I have for you does not come from the peace-prosperity, successful-ministry or victory-in-this-life promises. The end goal of teaching the message of grace is not to get people to fund our ministries, although our ministries are funded by those to whom we minister. I am not about to give you the grace key to the supernatural financial breakthrough you have always been waiting for. I would like to encourage you in a practical way. You might have a fearing, maybe a slightly confused heart at the moment, which is absolutely normal; your heart will heal by the balm of His love for you. I would like to encourage you in a way that you can feel loved by God and the pressures of ministry leave you forever.

I don't have the key to getting people to give you a lot of money, but I do have the key for true peace and life as God intended it. Grace is not the key to the financial funding you always dreamed would provide your income. Grace is the key to dreaming with God. Grace is the key to a godly life that includes the fruit of generosity in you and in all those who believe the truth. Grace is the influence of God on the human race, through what Jesus has done, exploding in strong emotions and life-giving thoughts in you.

I can imagine the fear the words in this book can instill in the hearts of those who have been teaching the traditional messages on tithing, sowing and reaping. This fear will tempt you to run away from the truth, but you will also be running away from the freedom the truth brings. As pastors, we have love for the people and for what God brings forth in the church. We would hate to see the work of God suffer and go through pain. We would like to limit the pain of correction as much as possible.

I have great compassion for anyone who has ministry income based on the law system. It will be very difficult for you in these times. You have bills to pay, salaries and missionaries to support, while it is all funded by the traditional system of tithing, sowing and reaping. What can you do? How will you go about this matter? You may be asking yourself what will happen if your people get a hold of this book. What if they see that you don't have a foot to stand on in teaching giving as you use to teach it? What if they stop all their giving? What if they become rebellious against you? What if the people you've taught, and given your life to, turn their backs on you, thinking you willfully misled them in what you taught them? How can you handle this problem?

A Brother in Jail -

One of the most common responses to the truth about money is to believe the truth in secret and just say nothing about it. The matter is almost treated like a brother in jail; you don't talk about it and seldom visit.

Well, that is one way you can handle the problem, and it is much better than continuing to teach the traditional messages. On the other hand, people will still have their hearts rooted in the old lies. Their subconscious minds will be plagued by guilt and fear about God and their financial future, **and so will yours**.

Just remaining quiet about the money is a temporal solution but not the answer to the problem. We want the life God intended to manifest in the lives of His people, don't we? Yes, we do! And I can assure you, it will not happen by just keeping quiet about the matter. That will only cause your heart to be in more turmoil. There has to be a way to communicate the truth effectively. You don't want to live in fear, wondering when the people in the fellowship are going to get a hold of the truth about money and start questioning you, do you? No! We want freedom! We want the life of the Divine Ones for ourselves and all our people.

I have had many leaders call me to say that the church is not ready for my teaching on money, although they admit that they know it is the truth! I have been told that the timing isjust not right. I understand the concern and that people might misunderstand the teaching. Some people might run away from giving altogether, and interpret the message in ways that don't set them free from the power of the flesh. Should that stop us from teaching the truth? Did Paul stop teaching grace on account of some not appropriating the message in a way that would be beneficial for them and others? No! Paul taught the truth and corrected those who misunderstood it.

Making sure they continue to give

The other option is to speak the truth, but while making sure people will give, by saying things like …

- "Tithing is fulfilled but sowing is still valid."
- "You don't *have* to tithe but you will *get* to tithe, if you are in grace."
- "You can give without love but you cannot love without giving."
- "The tithe is not an obligation, nor is sowing and reaping; yet, it is a special way to have more than what would normally be yours."
- "Under the law, you gave ten percent so grace will make you give *at least* ten percent."
- "Giving sets you free from stinginess."

Teachings like this will leave you and your people fear-bound. It does not possess the freedom to bring forth the life of God in the individual. We don't want to trick ourselves into thinking we are free, by having a belief that would allow these types of slogans. We want to be free and free indeed! Trying to keep a back door open for the law, hidden behind grace language, is not going to get you to the life God intended for us.

Healing for your heart

The best thing you can do, as a leader, is to ask God to persuade your heart about His love for you. You will have to come to the conclusion that God does not have you for the purpose of doing work for Him. He has you first and foremost as His friend. There is no quick fix for this or anything else in the Kingdom of God. All things are relationship based.

Maybe, like me, you also feel you've lost touch with your Abba, that your loving Father who said He would provide for you is dead. As preachers, we are just as influenced by what we preach as those who listen to us. If what we've preached has brought fear, guilt, and works-based giving to our people, we will be as deep into this death as they are, if not deeper. We preached it from the depth of our hearts and believed it ourselves, did we not?

When it comes to teaching the truth about money, setting people free from the power of the flesh could send shivers down your spine. Especially if it means you will have to stand up and tell the people that you were wrong in what you taught and have misled them.

When you open the container called, *faith in His provision apart from my contribution*, you might find it completely empty of strong persuasion. If this is you, I have good news for you! The Gospel does not *demand* faith but *supplies* faith. Let me say that again: God does not demand faith but supplies faith, as He manifests His equity of character to you in what Jesus has done for you. True freedom will start when you, from the depth of your heart, see and understand how God serves you today.

Entering into the union we have with God sets us free from self-preservation, since we are preserved in His eternal life. Self-preservation is one of the deadliest things in the Church, and it's the very fruit that manifests all kinds of unnecessary work for us as leaders. Many of the teachings and church programs we have are born from a fear of not having, born from a fear of failing, and born from a fear of the people leaving. There is freedom from all of those things. Self-preservation, which is born from a law-system economy, will make you implement large systems, with many staff members and programs, to keep your head above water. This is destroying many preachers and their members. The sadness of this destruction is that it is all in the name of obedience and Jesus. I am not against big at all; I am talking about the motive and foundation from where we live.

You will have to be very honest with yourself, and declare what you feel the motive of your ministry is to God. Let Him flood your heart with a revelation of peace and joy, to the point that belief is a fruit of knowing His love for you, and not a root that will give you the money you were dreaming of all your life.

As you read this book again—especially Part One—God will persuade your heart with thoughts about your union with Him, so that you will find your heart starts to believe in Him. Don't be in a hurry; talk to God and give Him time to persuade your heart. Your heart is not going to be brand new just because you heard some truth once. Your heart needs persuasion; your heart needs to see that it is safe to trust God. It can take a while before you see the true fruit of peace manifest in your life. The quickest way is to acknowledge the truth you have heard as the truth to people close to you, like your wife or some good friends, people you have trusted for a long time. And steer away from having doctrine that contradicts the nature of a good Father.

Take what I have said; take what encourages you of the truths in this book and speak to God about it. Speak to Him about it until you are not hearing *me* saying it anymore. Speak to God until you can hear *Him* saying it to you. As you hear Him teach you these truths, you will find doubt, fear and unbelief leave your heart. This is where His life starts to manifest in you. This is where you will find the peace that could allow you to boldly proclaim the truth, leading your people to a place where they can experience true generosity, a place where they experience God living in them as He lives in you. This generous, free life is what God has planned for us all!

It would be crazy for me to try and put my hand to a strategy on how you need to approach your church leaders, family or friends with this radical truth, which can cause some serious shakes in your circle of influence. All I can say is that it will take faith, not a faith that you decide to work up, but a belief that comes from an Abba who has won your heart. Please know that you are the leader of your people and that God will work in you both to will and to manifest the declaration of this truth to all!

My closing statement for this book is this:

I can promise you there will be those who misunderstand you. I can promise you that there will be people abusing what you say. I can promise you that you will experience persecution. But, I can also promise you that by embracing the truth, you will have many people who are set free as you believe and preach it. I can promise you that you will experience supernatural peace in the area of your finances, which is God-birthed. I can promise you grace-based provision. I can promise you that the fruit of contentment will flood your life.

With this being said, enjoy your new life that is God-filled, peaceful and fearless. Enjoy your life with our loving ABBA.

Prayer -

Father, my heart is flooded with gratitude towards You. I am grateful that, after nine years, I could put on paper what you have spoken to me in my inner man.

Thank you for loving us and giving us a place with You in the Godhead.

Your love and servant heart has brought me life. Your son and friend,

Bertie

Made in the USA
Lexington, KY
12 September 2019